DESTROYER MEN

Dedicated to the memory
of Victoria Harrison.

DESTROYER MEN

Early Memoirs of
Commander J.A.J. Dennis DSC RN
& Life of
Rear-Admiral J. Lee–Barber
CB DSO & Bars RN

Alec Dennis and Anthony J. Cumming

First published in Great Britain in 2020 by

Goodrington Publishing

ISBN 978 1 5272 5287 5

Printed and bound in England by Short Run Press, Exeter.
Short Run Press
25 Bittern Road
Exeter
EX2 7LW

Contents

ACKNOWLEDGEMENTS

Working with the son and daughter of the late Commander 'Alec' Dennis over the past few years has already given me the honour and pleasure of bringing their father's superb war memoirs to a wider readership. Thanks to their friendship and unstinting cooperation, I published these with my introduction and historical note as *In Action with Destroyers* back in 2017. Charity Reddington and Alan Dennis of British Columbia, Canada, have now made additional material available from their father's papers and provided most of the financial support for publication of a further book. For this I am enormously grateful. I must also mention our other financial backers, Sarah Lee-Barber and Norah Churton, who made generous contributions towards the production costs.

Sadly, Victoria Harrison, John Lee-Barber's daughter, died during the production of this book and I am indebted to her memory for obtaining copies of her father's service reports from the Ministry of Defence on my behalf. Victoria also lent me a number of books written by contemporaries and various other items that proved valuable research aids. Victoria's sister, Sarah, sent me some useful family insights and photographic images for which I am grateful. Caroline Kennard also kindly provided a photograph of John Lee-Barber that I have adapted for the dust jacket.

My grateful thanks also go to military intelligence historian Hugh Sebag-Montefiore, who lent me valuable help and encouragement. Hugh had previously interviewed Alec over Polares and his insights into a highly complex subject were invaluable.

Barnaby Blacker copy-edited the text with skill and sensitivity and our thanks go out to him and all those involved in the production process. Howard Davies and Judy Noakes of the National Archives, Kew gave essential copyright advice and the government material published in the appendices comes under the terms of the Open Government Licence: nationalarchives. gov.uk/doc/open-government-licence/version/3

Ben Clark of the Short Run Press, Exeter gave valuable assistance in bringing this book to print and my wife Sarah, played a key role in the production process liaising with Ben and transferring the manuscript into the final templates. Her support has proved invaluable.

Any mistakes transposing Alec's text in Part I or errors in other parts of the book are entirely my own responsibility.

Anthony J. Cumming, Paignton, 2019.

PREFACE

For those unfamiliar with his writing, John Alexander Jeffreys Dennis, better known to friends and colleagues as 'Alec', was a popular, brave, and dedicated naval officer with one of the broadest ranges of experience in the destroyer service of the wartime Royal Navy. Awarded the Distinguished Service Cross and Mentioned in Despatches three times, he served in four destroyers: *Griffin, Savage, Valorous* and *Tetcott*, the last two of which he commanded. Alec became one of the youngest first lieutenants in the Royal Navy and in 1944 probably the youngest officer to command a destroyer in wartime. Had post-war naval development taken a different course this promising sailor may have achieved flag rank and a place on the naval staff. Instead, disillusioned with social and political developments in the UK and poor promotion prospects in the Navy, he sought a new life of opportunity in Canada where he was to spend the rest of his life. This new book includes details of his early life and Alec's hitherto unpublished written statement that helps clarify the circumstances surrounding *Griffin*'s capture of the German armed trawler *Polares* in 1940. The incident is familiar to military intelligence historians of the Second World War and the book includes copies of official documents Alec obtained to investigate allegations made against both him and the captain of the *Griffin*, (reproduced in the appendices) along with his service reports. These have proved valuable sources of information.

Having published Alec's war memoirs with my short commentary and historical note as *In Action with Destroyers 1939–1945* in 2017, I was subsequently contacted by Victoria Harrison, daughter of the late Rear Admiral John (Johnny) Lee-Barber, and ultimately Alec's great friend. 'Johnny' was undoubtedly one of the best destroyer captains the war produced and Alec was fortunate to come under his command. Dennis was an able officer in his own right, but without Johnny's astute recognition of potential he may have missed the opportunity to rise through the ranks so rapidly at such a young age.

For his part, Johnny remained a seaman at heart throughout his naval career, and his antipathy to paperwork, was—Victoria maintained—the reason why he never joined the Naval Staff and his reputation remains in relative obscurity. As Alec made so many positive references to Johnny throughout *In Action with Destroyers*, his readers will already have formed an impression of a brave, charismatic, and respected captain. However, Victoria wanted me to write a full biographical account of her father's career, or at least cover his exploits in more detail than anyone has yet attempted. Unfortunately, Johnny never kept a diary or set down many of his experiences on paper and most of his contemporaries have now died. This precluded any possibility of a full biography, but by examining official reports, drawing upon snippets published by naval writers and talking to his family, I garnered enough material to write a useful supplement to this account of Alec's childhood and pre-war naval life.

It cannot be denied that Alec's pre-war memoirs do not contain the drama of the wartime adventures he shared with Johnny. Nevertheless, for anyone interested in 1930s British social history, pre-war naval development, or an observer's view of the early stages of the Sino-Japanese War of 1937–45, a fascinating read awaits as Alec retained his witty and irreverent take on people and events so ably displayed in his wartime memoir.

Since writing his memoirs (and long before any of it was published) Alec became aware of comment by military intelligence historians concerning the capture of the German armed trawler *Polares* in 1940—a milestone in the intelligence war. As *Griffin* played an important role in seizing and securing this valuable intelligence prize, the highlighting of two matters he felt 'rather told against me' prompted him to investigate matters on his own account. Alec then obtained copies of official reports from the National Archives at Kew (formerly the Public Records Office) and placed a written statement in his private papers explaining the situation in more depth. I have reproduced the key documents in the appendices so that readers can draw their own conclusions as to whether officers at Scapa Flow closed ranks against *Griffin* to protect their own reputations. Whatever the truth of the matter, and despite Alec finally receiving a Mention in Despatches for his conduct, it is clear from talking to their families that both men firmly believed the truth was suppressed.

For the rest of this book, I was grateful to have at my elbow the recollections of Harry Wardle's *Forecastle to Quarterdeck*.

Before he became an officer, Harry served under Alec and Johnny as a torpedoman and shared in their experiences aboard *Griffin*, with Johnny later writing the foreword to Harry's book. Valuable for a number of interesting and amusing anecdotes about Johnny's time with the 17th Destroyer Flotilla commanding the O-class destroyer *Opportune is Arctic Destroyers* written by G.G. Connell, an R.N.V.R. seaman promoted to First Lieutenant of the O-class destroyer *Obedient*.

This then, is the story of two destroyer men. It begins with Alec's account of his early life and pre-war career in Part I. This is followed by my account of Johnny's pre-war life in Part II, including the *Polares* incident and the sinking of the *Scharnhorst*. Summaries of their post-war service are in the epilogue.

PART I

The Memoirs of Commander J.A.J. Dennis
1918-1938

Edited by Anthony J. Cumming

TOUT COMPREHENDRE C'EST TOUT PARDONER

A few years ago, I wrote a narrative of my wartime life in the Royal Navy, covering the twenty years from 1938. I will now try to tackle from memory the twenty years before that time. I was born on February 18th, 1918, at Caversham near Reading in a house called, for some unknown reason, 'Toots'. It still stands today although Caversham has been swallowed up by Reading. There is no plaque on the wall to mark this great occasion. My father was in France in the Royal Army Medical Corps. He had been there almost continuously since the outbreak of war in August 1914. My mother, naturally, was in the house at the time – in those days they did not insist on babies being born in hospital. As far as I know I gave no trouble.

FOREBEARS

My father was the youngest but one of the nine children of a Paymaster-in-Chief in the Royal Navy. Clearly there wasn't much money to go around. Indeed, I have a letter from my great-grandfather commiserating with my grandmother that they were moving to Ireland without a manservant. My grandmother died in 1879 by exhaustion in yet another childbirth, aged only 42. My father was 4 years old and I suppose his upbringing was largely in the hands of his elder sisters with whom in later years he did not see eye to eye. But he remained a close friend of his

1

eldest brother, my Uncle John, 17 years older than him and a great influence on him – and me, as it turned out. After growing up in Plymouth, Hull and Southsea, he graduated as a Doctor of Medicine in Ireland and Edinburgh (the cheapest way in those days) in 1899. He joined the army at once for the Boer War and sent to South Africa where he told me he was captured by the Boers who treated him like a gentleman but took his horse. Liking the life, he stayed on in the army. He and my mother were married at St. George's, Hanover Square, in April 1914 and so had little time together before he went off to France in August. I think my mother must have been quite a 'catch' for him as her parents were very well off in those days. That is, of course, not to say that they weren't very fond of each other. My mother was the youngest of seven children. Unfortunately, she was always treated as such by her family and as one of my aunts once said. she 'never really grew up'. Sadly, for her, her father, who was very fond of her, died not long before her wedding. John Thomas Strange was a prosperous brewer whose family came from Berkshire where they had owned the brewery at Aldermaston for several generations so JTS was able to send his three sons to Charterhouse and his four daughters to Cheltenham Ladies College. I shudder to think what that would cost today. My mother was partial in a sentimental and utterly platonic way to some older men and especially clergymen and dons. Indeed, I was called Alexander after my godfather Alec Wollaston who was a noted explorer and Cambridge don. He went on the early expeditions to Mount Everest in the 1920s as naturalist. But in 1929 he was shot dead at King's College, Cambridge, by a crazed student (an unusual happening in those days) so I never got to know him.

I was also named John after my uncle and Jeffreys after my great-grandfather – the one who took Napoleon to Elba. Richard Gunning Jeffreys had joined the Royal Navy in November 1812 at the age of 13. He was serving in HMS *Undaunted* when she embarked the Emperor at St Raphael and transported him to Elba. My great-grandfather was midshipman of the boat which took Napoleon to the ship, and the great man is said to have commented on his red hair and patted him on the head with the words: 'Soyez brave, mon enfant'. All the officers were given mementos; RGJ received a gold watch chain, now I believe in the possession of one of the Jeffreys' descendants. He later spent time in Canada, based in Halifax, and retired as a Commander when promotion generally was at a standstill. His son-in-law, my grandfather, also served in the RN from 1844 to 1886, and my Uncle John from 1880 to 1918. Two of my father's sisters married naval officers who later became admirals – indeed, Aunt Netta married two of them (Craigie and Tudor, of whom more anon) and her daughter married another. So, with a connection going back well over 100 years it is not surprising that from birth I was 'destined' (at least by my family) for the navy.

Well, not long after I was born, the crisis of the war happened with the great German offensive of March 1918 which nearly won them the war. It was followed by the Allied (mainly British) offensive which brought the war to an end in November 1918. I don't believe my father got home in this period. In March 1919 he was sent to Cologne as part of the British Army of Occupation, but returned to England in July. He had volunteered to be seconded to the Army in India, where the pay and conditions were better. So we all set off on October 25th, 1919, from Liverpool to Bombay in the SS *Northumberland*.

With us came our wonderful Nanny, Miss Kate Williams, who stayed with my family for some forty years. As was the way in those days and circles, I was to see a lot more of her than of my parents (in the words of the song – 'always a mother, never a wife!'). I am grateful to her for giving me such a good start in the three Rs that I never found school at all difficult – academically, that is. My father as a lieutenant-colonel R.A.M.C. was in charge of a series of Military Hospitals in India – Bareilly, Wellington, Madras and Quetta. My earliest memories are of Wellington, near Ootacamund, where we lived in an attractive bungalow with a garden that was almost English. I used to watch my father shaving in the morning and, being interested (as now) in money, I asked him what he did with his. 'I put it in the bank,'

3

he said. There was a grassy bank behind the house and I spent some time fruitlessly trying to find the hiding place. I also remember being very much perturbed at the idea of the crucifixion which I suppose had been explained to me. My parent's yellowing photographs of those days show several rather masculine-looking men, typical of the Raj, in their tweed coats, hats and pipes. I have one of my father, sprightly, on a horse (I still have his riding breeches which I wore for years myself). He had a Chevrolet motor car with an Indian driver. In fact, I never saw either him or my mother driving a car. Another memory is of being in the car with him on the way back from the golf course when the first drops of rain of the monsoon fell. Great was the relief expressed at the end of the heat. I can still smell the sweetness of the water on the dusty road.

In May 1923 we left Bombay for Karachi in a horrible little ship called the *Linga*, and thence to Quetta where my brother was born on November 16th, 1923. My memories of that place mainly centre around playing with Indian boys in the grounds. But in February 1924 we set off for England for my father's six months leave. We travelled by train from Quetta to Karachi. I have vivid memories of the red orb of the sun setting in a wave of heat over the desert. I must have been a damned nuisance because I was thirsty and uncomfortable. The little whirring fan didn't do much good. On arrival at Karachi we boarded a ship and watched with interest the little Indian boys diving for coins thrown from the docks. I would have liked to do that. Then, the trip across the Indian Ocean to Suez where there were many ships waiting to go through the Canal including one with a bright green hull which for some reason remains vividly in my memory. My sixth birthday was celebrated on board, but somebody ate my cake. I got another one. It must have been on this passage home from India that my parents were at a fancy-dress party at which my father appeared as Tutankhamen, then all the rage, his tomb having been discovered a few months before. As a result, he (my father) found himself called 'Tootsie' by my mother and some close friends. It was odd that I'd been born in a house called 'Toots' long before the Pharaoh's tomb had been found.

ENGLAND ON MY OWN

Back in England, my parents rented a house in Southsea and I started to go to school at a nearby establishment run by a Miss Nightingale (or was it Nightingale Road?). In August 1924 my father was again appointed to the British Army of Occupation in Germany, but he seems to have got another appointment in India so in December my family sailed again for Bombay in the troopship *Assaye*, leaving me behind. This, of course, was the practice in those days. India was thought to be unhealthy for children, as indeed it had been for all ages in the last century, and an English education was considered to be essential. I ended up healthy and well educated but otherwise I don't think it did me any good.

AUNTS

I found myself 'farmed out' to various aunts, all of whom were kind to me but it wasn't the same as having one's own family. But at least I got to know many of my cousins (I had thirty first cousins!) quite well and have since enjoyed their company and friendship. At least I had a better time than Bobby Craigie, son of my cousin Leslie Craigie who became Ambassador to Japan in 1937. Young Bobby got left in the care of my aunt, his grandmother, who had become a tartar and he hated every moment of it. My father never got on with her so luckily I was never left in her tender clutches.

At first I stayed with my Aunt Beetle (Beatrice) who was my mother's sister and was married to an Australian called Clive Mort. They had one daughter, Helen, who was my age. We used to be taken for walks together and got along pretty well. They lived at Ryde, Isle of Wight, and one of my memories over several years is the sight of the great ocean liners such as the *Berengaria, Mauretania* and *Olympic* steaming majestically up or down the Solent; the great age of transatlantic travel by sea. One morning in 1927 I saw the new *Rodney* arriving at Spithead, little realizing that I was to serve in her nine years later. That was the day I trod on a piece of glass on the beach. It was most painful, took ages to heal and left a scar which is still there to remind me. I also stayed with my aunt Olive Illingworth at Bramley, Hampshire, with their four children. Uncle Charles was a large red-faced man who looked like a character from Pickwick Papers. He and my aunt hunted and lived very well getting through much of their money in the process. They were kind to me but their house was so cold that I dreaded going up to my bedroom. They had a summer house at Seaview. My uncle sailed a lot, having served in naval reserves during the war. All we cousins of my mother's family used to congregate there during the summers and quarrelled a lot. Another vivid memory is of watching the splendid 'J' Class yachts such as *Britannia* (raced by King George V), *White Heather, Lulworth* and so on, racing in the Solent, sometimes coming quite close inshore.

Then there was aunt Rose Stokes who lived at Alverstoke with her husband Alick, another retired naval captain, and their daughter Diana. With them I used to watch the fast seaplanes of the Schneider Trophy races, roaring round Fort Gilkicker winning the World Speed record at 330 or so mph. Lovely streamlined things they were, the shape of things to come in that the Spitfire was to some extent based on them by its maker, Supermarine. Another aunt who sometimes took me in was Marjorie Strange, married to Uncle Gerry, my mother's second brother. Gerry inherited the brewery because, I was told later, his older brother Percy had blotted his copybook by getting a servant girl in the family way and then marrying her. A lawsuit followed at the time of the First World War after Percy, in the trenches, not expecting to survive, had left his bride his portion of a trust. Apparently the lawsuit never came to a conclusion and is still open. Uncle Stanley, another brother, also married beneath him and I only met him once. So Gerry got the brewery and also lived very well and seems to have got through most of that money. Aunt Marge, a great personality, had an unlucky life in many ways. Her first-born son died at the age of 5, her second son 'Bunny' was killed in WW2 over Berlin in a bomber, and her brother, Rear-Admiral Ned Evans, was lost in an aircraft over the Atlantic about the same time. He had been serving in Ottawa, concerned with supplies in Canada, and became a great friend of Frank Ross, later Lieutenant-Governor of British Columbia. I wish I had known this when I came to British Columbia and met him. I know he would have given me a much-needed helping hand. My uncle Gerry was killed after World War Two in a freak accident when a bus ran up to the sidewalk outside St George's Hospital at Hyde Park Corner. The only child who survived was my cousin Pam, a little older than me, a lovely girl with startling auburn hair who became a dear friend. She too had some bad luck; her first marriage lasted a very short time and her second husband who was in every way ideal for her (he too had been in the navy during the war and had done well, one of the earliest reserves to get a destroyer command) died of cancer at a far too early age.

Lastly among the 'regulars' was my father's youngest sister (with whom, unlike the others, he was on good terms), Aunt Kathleen, married to Charles Keighley-Peach, a retired rear-admiral of truly Victorian appearance – heavy jowls, a big bald head and side-whiskers. He had a Clyno motorcar with a great many levers and a mica windscreen. Indoors he spent much time 'listening in' to a crystal radio set with headphones. This thing made all sorts of whistling and cracklings while he tried to tune in to 2LO, the London Broadcasting Station [only the second British radio station to regularly broadcast]. It seems like another world. Years later in the 1980s I took my visiting cousin Rowena, his daughter, to the Maritime Museum in Victoria, B.C. There on the walls was an old photograph – 1882 – of HMS *Swiftsure* in Esquimalt. Sitting on the deck was the unmistakable figure of Uncle Charles, then a midshipman. He looked much the same when he was an Admiral but with more hair on top of his head and less elsewhere. He had one son, Lindsey, then a sub-lieutenant in the Navy, and five daughters. Lindsey became a leading naval aviator, and distinguished himself in the Mediterranean flying the only Gladiator available to protect the fleet, for which he got the DSO, as had his father. His son Peter, later also in the Fleet Air Arm, got one in the Korean War. The girls were all older than me but the younger ones were fairly close and we had quite a lot of fun. This was the era of the Charleston, the Eton Crop, Jazz and long cigarette holders. The Keighley-Peach girls formed a Pierrot band with drums and banjoleles which I watched with fascination. The other memorable thing was being taken to Brooklands Motor Racing Circuit to see Henry Segrave race, he being a holder of the world speed record and a distant cousin of the K-P's. My aunt, who was rather a character, kept dozens of Bantams and a posse of Pekinese dogs who yapped a lot. She was very kind to me. The girls used to put things under my pillow when I went to bed and bet me that they could remove them in the night without waking me. They always won.

UNCLE JOHN

When I was a bit older, I used to stay with my uncle John, my father's eldest brother. He was even then a relic of another age though quite up-to-date in his thinking. He was born in 1858 before Darwin's *Origin of Species*, before the radio, anaesthetics and the telephone; still well in the age of the sailing ship. I believe there were still public executions in England and slavery in America in his lifetime. He had served in the Royal Navy since 1880 and in 1918 retired as a surgeon rear-admiral from Haslar Naval Hospital. While there, he told me he had been complimented by King Edward VII on his beard. He lived in a rented house at Beaconsfield with a housekeeper, never having married. He wouldn't have electricity, so the rooms were lit by gas, and at night one went upstairs carrying a candlestick to a bath heated by a 'geyser' and a cold bedroom.

As much as anyone he was responsible for my being pointed towards the navy; but although he had many stories about the 'old navy', he never told me much about his own career. I wish now that I had asked him. He had served in the Burma war in the 1880s when King Thebaw was toppled at Mandalay: also on the West and East coasts of Africa including the occupation of Suakin during the war with the Mahdi; and for a long spell in China during the days of the emperors. He should have written memoirs. Some of his stories were about some remarkable characters in the Victorian navy, such as: Pompo Heneage, Prothero the Good, Prothero the Bad, and one Buller, who was heard through his skylight walking up and down in his cabin, intoning the words: 'Buller, C.B.' A story about Pompo Heneage (not told by my uncle) concerned a time when he was captain of one of those old battleships – black hull, white upperworks, yellow funnel and very low freeboard. She was going up the Thames and discomfited a Thames barge with the wash of his bow wave. As the barge passed down the side, the bargeman was heard to shout: 'Tell your captain to put on a clean shirt as I'm coming aboard to f**k him.' Down came the reply. 'Tell that bargeman to stick a rowlock up his arse and scull himself ashore.' Nowadays there'd be a lawsuit.

SCHOOL

Although all these relatives were pleasant enough to me, I found the constant change of 'home' upsetting, and these years weren't happy ones. It wasn't long before I was packed off to boarding school. It was quite a nice little pre-prep school called Melbreck at Tilford near Farnham. I started there in January 1925 just before my 7th birthday. I seem to have done well academically thanks to my good start with Nanny Williams. All I can remember of it was the headmaster, a Mr Fernie, and his wife and the nearby moorland where we played at being boy scouts in the heather. In my last term in the summer of 1926 I was suddenly overcome by acute appendicitis. I remember having a pain and being noticed by Mr Fernie after a game looking rather white. A doctor arrived and evidently it was decided that an immediate operation was necessary – there and then. Nearby, in Seale, lived my wonderful 'honorary aunt', Violet Mayo-Robson, who had been at school with my mother. Aunt Violet was the daughter of Sir Arthur Mayo-Robson, a most distinguished surgeon who I believe was an honorary physician to King George. Anyhow he was summoned and took out my appendix on the school table. I remember vividly the horrible sieve-like contrivance which was put over my face to administer the chloroform; the unsympathetic nurse who told me it was nonsense when I complained that I felt an anchor at the bottom of my bed; and the offending appendix shown me in a bottle. Nasty though it was, I was luckier than my brother. Some years later he also had appendicitis, but the doctors wrongly diagnosed tuberculosis so that he spent several months and a lot of my parent's money at a sanatorium in Switzerland. I believe they had to sell the silver. When he returned, apparently cured, the trouble erupted again and this time my father became convinced that it lay in the appendix. Eventually he insisted on an operation, was proved right, after which Alan was never ill again. It is odd that nowadays one seldom hears of appendicitis. In any case, I convalesced at Melbreck, watching the red squirrels (now extinct in that area) out of the window before going to the K-P's on holiday. From there I went, barely recovered, in September 1926, to a regular boy's preparatory school called Charters Towers at East Grinstead in Sussex.

PREP-SCHOOLS

I was there until the summer of 1930 when it merged with a school in Bournemouth called 'Saugeen'. Charters Towers, was

I believe typical of many boys' boarding schools in England in those days. I hated it. The poor food, the cold, the tendency to bullying by the older boys and reliance on the cane to maintain discipline and encourage learning was a poor return for high academic standards. The headmaster, a Mr Alderson, was an unsympathetic character and a bit of a sadist. I hadn't been there long when he informed me that 'a man wrapped up in himself makes a small parcel.' Unhelpful.

Some of the masters weren't bad – especially the ex-service ones. S.E. Axton, an axed naval officer, was a nice man who taught me mathematics well. Major Forsyth taught me how to shoot a rifle. 'Easy as pie, isn't it?' On the other hand, a Belgian called M. Buisseret, with bad breath, had no control over his classes and had to suffer reminders that the Belgians ran away at the Battle of Waterloo – whether it was true or how we knew, I don't know. At that time, I was unaware that one of my forbears had removed Lord Raglan's arm (or was it leg?) after the battle. An impatient piano teacher soon lost me because he was inclined to swipe at your fingers with a ruler if you made a mistake. But I've often regretted that I didn't have guts enough to keep it up. Memories include tedious hours standing in a row doing choir practice for Sunday service when we used to troop up Baldwin's Hill to a chapel where Mr Alderson read the lessons. He was proud of his sonorous voice and used to sing a version of 'Who Killed Cock Robin?' with lines much expanded for heavy humour, as in: 'Who will read the sermon? I, said the owl with my little Revised Version with notes, appendices and maps – first published at one shilling – but now reduced to tenpence ha'penny – I'll read the sermon.' Ending on a deep bass note. There weren't more than about 35 boys at the school, and I had no friends. I do remember two Indian boys, sons of a Rajah who used to visit them in his Rolls Royce. They were called Kashipur Raja Kumar, and Kashipur Kumar. Rumour had it that they had different mothers. We weren't very nice to them and I wonder what on earth they made of it. They both played cricket very well – a sport I came to loathe after being pressured into it.

At the end of each term the joy of release was tempered by the fact that I had to have all four wisdom teeth removed – one at the end of each term. I stopped off in London to have it done. In those days It was an unpleasant experience, done under gas and one felt awful for a long time afterwards. But I suppose it saved me from buck teeth. Another memory – a bit of history – is of hearing the great airship R101 flying overhead in the dark on her maiden voyage to India. She crashed in France later that night, and that put an end to British airship development. Next door to the school was an ancient mansion called Cromwell Hall. This was reputed to be haunted. Strange lights were to be seen moving about in the grounds. Scared as a small boy can be, I ran for my life along a covered way in the dark when detached alone from evening class to go to the main house for the weekly long bath.

MY PARENTS RE-APPEAR

In the late autumn of 1928, my parents reappeared, having been away nearly four years. I barely knew them. It had happened that my father at the age of 53 had not been selected for promotion above his present rank of lieutenant-colonel, R.A.M.C. I suspect that serving in India, rather than at home under the eye of those who mattered, may have told against him. Normally he would have served on for several more years before being retired, but he received a severe blow when he was informed that due to cut-backs and economies he was required to retire early at the end of 1928. This must have been most awkward as he still had my brother and myself to educate and he had no capital with which to purchase a practice. He was therefore obliged to accept an offer in the recruiting service of the army, examining recruits at Liverpool. The decision seemed both unfair and arbitrary particularly in view of his service record. Judging by some rather sad correspondence which my mother passed on to me, he tried hard, pulling every available string, to have the decision reversed, but to no avail. So back home they came in the troopship *Nevasa* in which by coincidence I was to travel to Malta eleven years later.

My parents came to see me at school in the middle of the autumn term. They stayed at a hotel nearby in Felbridge and we had a rather awkward reunion. Both my mother and father smoked cigarettes incessantly. I once calculated that between them they must have smoked a million of them in their lifetimes. I have a vivid memory of sitting in the hotel room with my father, looking over my stamp collection, he with a cigarette in his mouth. I fear I must have found them to be strangers and probably treated them as such. Of course, I had no idea of the problems of trying to bring up boys on meagre pay plus what he was to get from the recruiting job. My mother received some income from her shares in the brewery, but she never knew how much the dividends would be or when they would be paid. I think her brother deliberately kept her in the dark. I find it ironic that qualified doctors nowadays are considered very well off. So up to Liverpool they went, and decided to buy a house at West Kirby, a seaside resort on the Wirral Peninsular about half an hour's train ride from Liverpool. Actually, it wasn't half a bad place, healthy, open, by the sea with lots of facilities.

From my parent's point of view the main problem was that most of the local people had quite a different background, being 'north country', remote from the armed forces and largely involved in business. The congenial ones were mostly too rich to keep up with. We never ran a motor car, for example. However, I think my parents settled down to it, made some good friends and played a lot of bridge and golf, so it can't have been too bad. After a spell in an enormous 'hydropathic' hotel (since demolished) we moved into a modest but comfortable house in Claremont Road, West Kirby, where my parents stayed until 1945. We had a cook and a maid, Annie Thredgold, who stayed a long time. But this must have seemed a meagre staff after India. It can't have helped matters when my brother had to be sent to Switzerland as mentioned earlier.

CHANGE OF SCHOOL

In the middle of 1930 there was an improvement in my situation. My prep school at East Grinstead was feeling the pinch of the depression. Numbers fell, so the school merged with 'Saugeen'. The whole atmosphere was better. The new joint headmaster, E.A. Tregoning, was a civilized man who treated the boys with understanding and consideration. For a year there I was as happy as could be expected in a boy's boarding school and did just as well, if not better, academically. I even played cricket and started to learn Greek which I enjoyed, having hated Latin. Old Tregoning made Greek come alive with his stories of Greek myth and history illustrated with pieces of pottery taken from the Acropolis at Athens. I made friends with a boy called J.A.J. Ormrod whose family were kind to me at the weekends. About the only thing I remember about Bournemouth is seeing my first traffic lights, then a novelty.

THE VITAL DECISION

In my final term in the summer of 1931 I took examinations for two possible futures. I went up to Clifton College near Bristol to sit for a scholarship. I did achieve one, though not the top one I was aiming for. In the same term I also tried for the Royal Naval College, Dartmouth, and, of course, a naval career. I sat at the top of the Avon gorge at Clifton, looking at the suspension bridge and waterway and wondering which it should be. Family propaganda had seen to it that the issue wasn't really in doubt. I don't regret my choice of the navy but I've sometimes wondered how the career, probably academic, would have turned out. In any case I would have found myself in the navy in the war, but as a reserve officer, I suppose. The selection for the R.N.C. Dartmouth consisted of three parts: medical, academic and personal interview. At this time, when the Depression of the

14

thirties was well underway, the competition was severe. I believe there were over 400 applicants for 32 places. The medical weeded out a good many. Afterwards we liked to think of ourselves as perfect physical specimens with 20/20 eyesight. My parents had even worried about my webbed toes though some might feel these an asset in a seagoing person. Anyhow I had no problem with this one and went on to the academic exams. Like all these phases, this one was held in London. I remember only the French Oral which went well as must have done the rest of it, as I passed top of all those who had got this far. There remained the dreaded interview. As a little boy of 13 one went up interminable stairs in a building in Queen Anne's Mansions to be faced by a group of what seemed like ancient men seated round a table. We had been filled with gruesome stories of catch questions one might expect, such as the number of your taxi or how many stairs you had just mounted. Not that the reply mattered; rather, the way you tackled it. Some kind person had told me about one favourite question which entailed arriving at a 5-road crossroads where the signpost had blown down. It was lucky that I was indeed confronted with that very question. What would you do? Put the sign back up, I said demurely, with the correct arm pointing to the town you had come from. A kindly old man asked whether it would really be necessary to put the sign up again. A moment's thought produced the answer: 'no, sir you could work it out'. And I felt much more confident thereafter. In those days a middle-class background and accent, and especially naval connections, seem to have counted a lot – a *sine qua non* even; things have changed since. In due course I was, or perhaps my parents were, informed that I had passed. The choice – Dartmouth or Clifton – was put to me and of course it was to be the navy.

ROYAL NAVAL COLLEGE, DARTMOUTH

The summer holidays were occupied with being fitted out with a small naval cadet's uniform and preparing for a naval career. On September 23rd, 1931, we thirty-two little boys assembled on the platform at Paddington Station *en route* to Dartmouth. Somewhat ominously it happened to be the week of the famous mutiny at Invergordon [actually 15-16th September] where many sailors refused duty because of some unfeeling and badly handled cuts in pay. Even more significantly it was only five days after the Japanese army marched into Manchuria, ushering in the new era of aggression which came to a climax in World War Two and involved us all. I was accompanied by Uncle John who seemed to know several of the other parents or relatives who were also naval men. Feeling very strange in our unaccustomed uniforms and somewhat nervous we got into the train for the long journey to the West Country. We arrived at Kingswear on the River Dart and embarked on the ferry across the river, then up the hill to the rather imposing red and white college which was to be our home for the next three years and two terms.

LIFE AT DARTMOUTH

Much has been written about the Dartmouth of those days, but I suppose it is worth mentioning some of my own recollections and impressions.[1]
The cadets were divided into eleven 'terms', each named after a naval worthy of the past; Rodney (my term), Hood, Benbow, Anson, Exmouth, Grenville, Hawke, Blake, Drake, St. Vincent, Duncan. No Nelson and no modern name. The cadets of each term stayed together throughout its passage up through the ranks of seniority from First to Eleventh term. There was virtually no mixing between terms except to some extent in sports teams, so that each group became very close and assumed

16

a character of its own. Most became lifelong friends. Our Rodneys, the smallest ever, numbered 32 at the start and regarded ourselves as rather a tough lot. This impression was fostered by our winning the junior year rugby football competition against the two terms older than ourselves. There seem to have been 'other reasons', to be referred to later. The whole college, then, consisted of some 400 cadets ranging in age from 13½ to 17½. The senior years provided two 'cadet captains' in charge of each term, rather in the manner of prefects, under the guidance of a term officer who was a regular lieutenant or lieutenant-commander, usually thought to be specially selected as an example to be looked up to and emulated, as indeed many of them were. The naval staff consisted of these term officers and paymaster, engineer, medical and instructor officers headed by the commander and the Captain of the College, an august figure whom one normally saw only at a distance. In my first year this was Captain Sydney Meyrick who was relieved by Captain R.V. Holt, both of whom became Admirals. Parallel to these were the 'masters', or academic staff who taught the normal school subjects — English, Mathematics. Science, French and History (which had a strongly naval bias). In addition, we were instructed in Seamanship, Engineering and Navigation by the naval staff. Looking back, I can't help feeling that these were some of the best jobs in the lower academic world - small classes, select pupils, agreeable surroundings and few, if any, disciplinary problems. However I doubt if the pay was very good. Classes were indeed small - about ten in the senior years - and discipline was pretty tight. I think in fact that we got a very sound education, at least in the basics, though some of it was in a sense narrow, being directed towards converting us into a certain type of efficient and rather unquestioning naval officer. Many years later at a university in Canada I found this background to be invaluable.

KEMPSON

The headmaster, Eric W.E. Kempson, was another formidable figure in academic gown, mortarboard and monocle. His daughter, Rachel, later became an actress, married Michael Redgrave and was the mother of Vanessa, the somewhat Trotskyite and leader of left-wing political causes. One wonders where she picked up her fanaticism. I remember Rachel well because she was a beautiful girl and we suffered from complete seclusion from the fair sex. In our seventh term our dormitory overlooked, to some extent, the headmaster's garden where she could be seen sunbathing. Rumour (graded D6) had it that one of the engineer officers, frustrated in love, had cut his throat in the barber's shop. There were no other girls about – indeed very few women, apart from the Matron and some nursing sisters in the sick quarters, and Mrs Larter, the canteen manager's wife, an unprepossessing lady known as 'the Hag'.

MASTERS

Each cadet had a nominal 'tutor' who was supposed to look after his educational well-being. Mine was A.M.C. Nichol, a science teacher. He made no impression on me at all. Of the other masters, I remember Phil Bishop who taught us French. I met him thirty years later in Ontario, still teaching French, now at Trinity College School, Port Hope. He looked just the same. Then there was Mark Sugden, a famous Rugby international scrum-half whom I tried to emulate without success. He died in 1990. J.S. Sampson, who taught history, had a passion for heraldry and ancient siege warfare. His room was full of model medieval engines of war such as trebuchets with which one was occasionally allowed to bombard the battlements on the walls. 'Daddy' Milne, another science teacher, lingers in the memory for remarking in his thick Scottish accent with pawky humour, at the beginning of a new class: 'Dear, dear. Two Hoares in our class.' Then there was 'Piggy' Reid who owned a fine yacht called the *Black Adder* in which he used to take boys for a sail. He had, I suspect, a bit of a weakness for them, never I'm sure carried into practice. 'I like freckly knees,' he said to me once as we were sailing off the River Dart. I was feeling seasick but didn't realise that this affliction would plague me throughout my career at sea.

NAVAL INSTRUCTORS

The Naval Instructor officers taught us Navigation which included Spherical Trigonometry as a background to sun and star sights. I found it tricky to grasp, and it was never used in practice when we got to sea. The Engineers presided over a complex at Sandquay down by the river, reached by hundreds of steps. I knew them well having had to run down and up them as a reprisal for yawning at gym. Here we learnt the rudiments of marine engineering, together with some very basic skills which included engineering draughtsmanship, making a wooden dove-tailed ditty Box, a tempered spring, a case-hardened chisel and a cast brass door knocker in the shape of a galleon. Some of us still have theirs. I also skinned my knuckles cutting a groove in a hunk of brass which refused to go straight. I soon came to the conclusion that I wouldn't make much of an engineer, though I enjoyed the drawing office which was run by a civilian pensioner with a nasal stoppage and not much sense of humour. He had some difficulty preserving discipline, his frequent complaint being 'You yug gedlemen have'd cub here to abuse yourselves.'

In our senior year, the top ten or so academically were assigned to the 'Alpha' class, in which more of a university approach was taken, with lectures and self-study. It took me a while to adjust to this, being lazy by nature. I had always been top of the term academically, but I slipped a bit towards the end and only passed out third in the final exams, thus missing having the letters R.R. after my name in the Navy List for ever after. My father was not pleased. Nor was I. However, I did get the prize in Mathematics and English which I felt were the ones that mattered. Actually, I had chosen the science specialization, which I think was a mistake. I'd have done better in languages and in the long run they would have been more useful. For some reason we studied French history 1815 to 1870 in considerable detail. Great emphasis was, of course, placed on physical fitness and team games. Numbers in my day being small, I managed to achieve the First XV at rugby football and the First XI at soccer, but was far from outstanding. I wouldn't play cricket in the summer and went sailing instead. I also played squash (a lot) and tennis (a little) and, in the senior years, golf at Churston. Every day you had to record your physical exercise in a log and a certain minimum had to be achieved. An organized game counted in full, as did a long-distance run. Swimming, rifle shooting or a shorter run counted half, and so on. There is no doubt that we were very fit. I remember running through pretty Devonshire countryside, feeling on top of the world and saying to myself: 'How happy I am!'

This was in spite of the strict and sometimes petty discipline which surrounded us. But we knew where we stood and I think it was, at least, fair. A minor transgression such as lateness or a button undone on parade would probably result in a tick in a book kept by the cadet captain. When you had achieved three of these (five in your first year or so) you would be summoned after 'lights out' to the lobby at the end of the dormitory. The list of your crimes would be read out. 'Have you anything to say?' 'No excuses' would be followed by three strokes of the cane whereupon you nipped smartly back to bed, relieved you had three ticks ahead on a clean sheet. You got to know the ropes pretty well and I think I was only flogged once or twice. Of course, in your senior year if you were a cadet captain (as I was) you did the beating. Why we didn't all become little sadists I don't know. I certainly cut notches in my cane to register the number of my victims. To my shame, on one occasion I managed to get myself out of an awkward situation which would have resulted in a beating (two ticks on the sheet). I told a barefaced lie and stuck to it. I had been reported as 'improperly dressed' (i.e. in the wrong rig) somewhere or other, and I absolutely denied being the person reported. The investigation went up the scale to my Term Officer. The stakes rose but under some pressure I stuck to my story and in the end got away with it on the grounds that my word as an officer cadet must be accepted. Hence the shame. But I still feel sneakily pleased at not weakening. There's a moral somewhere.

Our treatment was odd in some ways. We were, of course, young gentlemen and potential officers. Therefore we had servants to do our laundry and polish our boots. Mine was a real old west country character called Tom Pillar with a wonderful thick accent which might have been like Sir Francis Drake's. But we had to fold our clothing and display it on the front of our sea chests in immaculate style, each item in its regulation place and lined up to the millimetre. We had to spend a lot of time lining up all the sea chests themselves so they were in perfect alignment for 'Rounds' – a feat more difficult than it sounds. One certainly learnt to be neat and tidy. I still am. As for privacy, each chest had a small lockable 'private till'; that was all. 'Rounds' were the traditional parade around the establishment at 'lights out' by the Duty Officer preceded by a regulating petty officer carrying a lamp and followed by other functionaries such as the cadet captain. One lay at attention in bed, all shoes up alongside, and was assailed by an expensive aroma of port or brandy, it being the end of dinner time in the wardroom.

Other old-timers on the pensioner's list were headed by Chief Petty Officer Mitchelmore, our Term Chief, who met us on arrival at Kingswear and was a sort of 'Sea-daddy' to the term. He was said to have eleven children and was working on another to complete a cutter's crew. He and an old boy called Tugee who ran the seamanship room seemed to exude a scent of cut tobacco, spun yarn and tarred hemp. I am sure they had served in the days of sail in Queen Victoria's navy. They taught us knots and splices, anchor work, boat work and a host of naval terms

21

from keelson to mainbrace. There was also a pensioner's band, to whose martial music we marched at divisions. Our very first term they had replaced a Bluejacket's band, a sign of the economic times. Some of them looked shrunken, such as Harry Oke who wasn't much bigger than his trombone.

ROUTINES

The weekdays started early with a bugle call, the Reveille at 0600. The requirement was to go through a cold salt-water plunge. This was not pleasant in winter and one had to weigh the chances of getting away with skipping through barely wet, or getting a tick for shirking. Then, ship's biscuits and hot cocoa before the first academic classes at 0700, at which time a sleepy master was not at his best either. After breakfast there was the morning parade – Divisions – at which the colours were hoisted and a prayer was said (Roman Catholics fell out and did their own thing behind the wall). When detailed to hoist the ensign one had to time it carefully so as to reach the top of the hoist exactly with the last notes of the anthem. Then we marched past and dispersed to morning classes. We always moved between classes at the double, sometimes clutching a pile of books under one arm while saluting passing officers and masters with the other.

Some masters, tired of lifting their arms up and down in acknowledgment, rather wearily kept one hand raised as they walked along, occasionally wiggling their fingers. Roland Plugge told me years later that he failed to give an adequate salute to Lieutenant-Commander St John Cronyn, an irascible gentleman of the old school with a fine command of invective (e.g. 'eyes like two poached eggs in a sea of blood...'). 'What's your name boy?' 'Plugge, Sir'. 'Well, go and ------- pull yourself.' Only fairly cultured. One rarely arrived late for anything. My French master, should this happen, made you stand to attention and intone, 'Je regrette infiniment arriver en retard. Jamais je ne le ferais plus. J'ai fait tout le chemin à la course at je suis hors d'haleine.' (I'm infinitely sorry I'm late. I'll never do it again. I've done the whole race and I'm out of breath.) Well at least I learnt one useful phrase.

Our normal dress in the mornings was: reefer jacket with lanyard, white flannel shirt and black tie, uniform cap, white flannel trousers (hard to keep clean) and boots. In the evenings we wore blue uniforms. Cadet captains wore a gold badge on the right cuff and term cadet captains wore a star above it. The two chief cadet captains wore the badge on each cuff and had privileges such as a private study and the meals were served (after a fashion) in the large and quite imposing mess hall. Here we would sit together as a term at the long mess tables.

The food was whisked around by pensioners who pushed it on wheeled trolleys. Two of them stay in memory. Jehu who, like his namesake, drove his trolley furiously; and Isaiah, one of whose eyes was, of course, higher than the other. On the whole the food was pretty good – a great deal better than prep school fare – but there were dishes which were cordially disliked, named 'baby's bottom' and 'nigger s..t'. We used to line up by terms in the halls, and march into meals. We took so much exercise that we were ravenously hungry, so at teatime, when buns were laid out, one to a place, the first ones in went along the table grabbing as many buns as possible. Late comers lost out. Hence the name of the meal: the 'bun rush'. But there was always unlimited bread and jam to fill up.

CRISIS

About the middle of our first term we Rodneys were suddenly hauled in front of the captain, that august figure whom we normally saw only at a respectful distance. Captain Sydney Julius Meyrick (whose son many years later was my captain in the *Savage*) later went on to be an admiral and C. in C. West Indies; but at this moment he was severity itself and, I suspect, a little worried. We were given dire warnings that certain forms of bullying must cease forthwith, or we would be 'OUT'. I had absolutely no idea what he was talking about. However, the story soon came out. It appeared that some of the rougher members of our term had taken it into their heads to bully those who were Admiral's sons – notably Domvile and Somerville. John Somerville bore it with fortitude though I don't think he ever forgave Dartmouth, and left the navy soon after the war for another distinguished career. *After reading this, John told me that this gave the wrong impression. He did well in the navy but had to retire to manage the estate after his father died, as an Admiral of the Fleet.*

But young Domvile's father happened to be Second Sea Lord and Chief of Naval Personnel, a man of vast influence to all careers, including that of the captain. Anyhow, hell broke loose and I suppose that thereafter the bullying ceased. Poor Domvile didn't last long actually. He was a nice enough lad – I slept next to him as we were of course arranged in alphabetical order; probably he had only mentioned the matter in his weekly letter to his mother. He was withdrawn at the end of the term and went to that *avant-garde* co-educational establishment at Dartington Hall, not far away. Years later when I was long retired in British Columbia, I met his widow. He had been living on Lasqueti Island near Vancouver Island and had, I was told, been operating a general store in this sparsely populated and agreeable spot. One evening after dark he had set off with his two sons in a fast motor boat to Nanaimo to fetch some provisions. Neither the boat nor the occupants were ever seen again. It was assumed that they had hit a 'deadhead' and sunk at once in those cold waters. Sometime earlier, in 1971, Norman Macpherson had written to Domvile to ask if he would care to attend a 40th reunion of the term's survivors. Not surprisingly he replied rather testily that he wasn't about to travel some 8,000 miles to meet some people who had given him a rough time all those years ago. They were a strange family. Admiral Domvile had served as Director of Naval Intelligence and became convinced that Britain's future lay in friendship with the

Germans. He stuck to this view even after the rise of Hitler and became a prominent member of the LINK, an Anglo-German association. Thus in 1940 he was interned in prison by Winston Churchill along with Oswald Mosley and others with like sympathies.

In our junior terms we were harassed quite a lot by the cadet captains in attempts to 'smarten us up'. One threat, put into practice once or twice, was that of a 'STRAFE', an expression which must have survived from the First World War. For this, the term was assembled in the gunroom (each term had a sort of assembly/recreation room, so called). We were then required to do certain things at the rush, such as changing into sports rig, running to the gymnasium and back and changing into something else, all with the threat of dire punishment for the last one to make it. It was a form of hazing now perfected by the Americans and rather barbaric, though it did teach one the skill of making rapid changes of clothes, a useful accomplishment in naval life. In many other ways we were treated with consideration and I have no doubt that officers and masters were dedicated to making future naval officers of us.

WATER SPORTS

We spent a fair amount of time in boats on the River Dart. There were 'Blue Boats', small rowing boats for two or three, and sailing dinghies in which races were held in the tricky conditions of the pretty river where fickle winds blew down the valleys and around the hulks of disconsolate merchant ships laid up because of the Great Depression. These included some large liners such as the *Oropesa* from the South American routes. We were actually taught to sail in 27' whalers and 32' cutters, the latter quite heavy when manned with a full crew. Norman Macpherson succeeded in ramming a pontoon full tilt in a fresh breeze, having put the tiller over too late. Nobody seemed to mind much. There were also two yachts attached to the college:

the *Amaryllis* which had a long racing record and the *Tai-Mo-Shan* which had been sailed back to England from Hong Kong by an enterprising group of submariners in the days when this was unusual. [In 2008 the *Tai-Mo-Shan* starred in the film *Mamma Mia*! directed by Phyllida Lloyd).] In our senior summer we much enjoyed taking diesel-engine motor boats right up the Dart to Totnes where one could risk a drink or two of 'scrumpy'. Other seagoing entailed trips to Start Bay in the attached coal-burning minesweeper *Forres*, mainly for instruction in coastal navigation. And on one memorable occasion we had a day at sea in the aircraft carrier *Courageous* and watched take-offs and landings by her primitive looking aircraft. I remember a hearty breakfast at which some cadet consumed with relish a senior officer's personal marmalade, causing some nausea.

FARMS AND RELIGION

On Sunday afternoons in our more senior years we were allowed to visit local farms. Small groups of four or five would adopt a farm a few miles away, where we would keep a gramophone and records. It was joyful to relax, sleep, fool around and play the records after an enormous tea with fried eggs, jam and Devonshire cream. We all smoked cigarettes, some pipes, illegally of course. Then we returned to the college much refreshed in mind for evensong in the chapel. I still remember the smell of nicotine on my fingers folded in prayer.

As for religion, of course we attended morning service every Sunday after divisions and inspection. The chapel was a fine one, done in white with a large model of Drake's *Golden Hind* hanging above the nave. Occasionally a distinguished bishop would preach and I remember especially the Bishop of Exeter, one of the mighty Cecil family clad in purple and bearded like the pard – an apostolic figure. At age 16 or so we were all confirmed into the Church of England – in alphabetical order, except Francis Fouke and Paul Pierano, our two R.C.s. There were no other religions, denominations, agnostics or atheists. Life was simple in those days; we were a homogeneous lot; all white and male. Religious instruction was given by the padre, the Reverend Norman Kent, who had a distinctive manner of speech emphasising his terminal 'T's which made him rather a figure of fun. We heard a lot about his experiences in HMS *Glasgow* in 1914-15 when after the Falklands battle she searched for the escaped German cruiser *Dresden* among the fjords and inlets of the coast of Chile. This was more interesting than Balaam and his ass. Another aspect of religious instruction entailed learning by heart two substantial pieces of the Old and New Testaments and then declaiming them from the pulpit in the chapel which was empty except for the formidable figure of E.W.E. Kempson, the headmaster who sat in judgement in the back row. He wore a monocle and if it dropped from his eye in the course of your oration you knew it wasn't going well. There was a prize but none of us was considered good enough for it. I will say that after that experience I never again felt stage-fright when called to speak in public. And I can still quote 'David and Jonathan were lovely and pleasant in their lives...' and 'Though I speak with the tongues...' and 'Remember now thy creator in the days of thy youth...' So, it was worth the trouble.

TERM OFFICERS

Our Term Officer was responsible for other aspects of our development and well-being. First, we had Colin Wauchope who went on to be relieved by Harry Sharpe who didn't stay long – something to do with the economy cuts. Then there was Edward Cooper who spoke very rapidly in a rather high-pitched voice. He once remarked on my hair as being 'rather poetical'. It can't have been very long by modern standards. His brother George looked almost identical and served with me later, having survived being a Japanese prisoner of war. Lastly there was

Wully Wood, a fine-looking man who had been an international rugby footballer. Wully had to give us our 'sex lectures' and very odd some of them seem to have been. Sadly a few years later he turned out to have been a pederast and, when found out, shot himself in his cabin in the *Rodney.* But at the time he was with us he was considerate and a good example. The fact that the terms were virtually segregated from each other, the busy schedule and fairly close supervision meant that there seems to have been very little of the sort of juvenile homosexuality so prevalent in many public schools of the time. But it is a fact that we saw so little of the opposite sex that they seemed to me in those days to belong to another race.

This must have seemed quite extraordinary to one cadet in particular. This was Don Juan of Spain, son of King Alfonso XIII who had been deposed. I remember the king visiting the college in our early days in 1931-32 and thought I detected a faint rising of the royal eyebrows as he watched us cadets dancing together on a Saturday evening. (This was meant to help us become more socially versatile in spite of the lack of partners of the right sex.) On this occasion we dared Ralph Drummond to go up to the king and ask him to dance, but sanity prevailed. in spite of this curious aberration, the king did send Don Juan to the college for a year when, a lot older than the rest of us, he seemed to go his own way and was reputed to 'leap over the wall' from time to time to live up to his name with the ladies of the town. Not likely, really. In spite of it all he became an anglophile. General Franco didn't approve of him so he never became king, and stood aside in favour of his son Juan Carlos who is now on the throne. Another royal personage appeared in my senior year. At the end of each term there was a dance, one of the few occasions when real girls appeared in the sacred precincts. This time we were honoured by the presence of the Prince of Wales (later King Edward VIII and Duke of Windsor), himself an ex-cadet. He was at this time entangled with Mrs Simpson.

28

LAST DAYS

In my last two terms I became first a cadet captain and then a term cadet captain and found life most agreeable. I had charge of the Drake term, a year our junior, and regret to say that I was pleased to chastise, for some irregularity, the young Roger Keyes, son of the famous admiral; an insufferable lad, now I believe the second Lord Keyes. In our last term the two 'leaders' were made chief cadet captains. These were Norman Macpherson and Peter Keith-Welsh. Norman left the Service early, having married Joan Backhouse, the First Sea Lord's daughter, and Peter went on to be a captain. In general, the cadets fulfilled their promise and many, but not all, became distinguished admirals.

Throughout my time at Dartmouth I was very fit and only once succumbed to an illness. I had injured my knee (contusion of the right patella) playing hockey. I took it down to the sick bay where I was asked if I had ever had measles. No, I hadn't. So, I was sent into a room where two cadets were exuding measles from every pore. In due course I got it too. Naval medicine? Though arbitrary, perhaps it was a good idea to get it over, but I was angry at the time as it affected my academic work at a tricky moment, especially in mathematics. We were just starting calculus, and having missed the introductory lectures, I never really grasped it. However, we all had a great time in the sick quarters where large numbers of us went through the disease. After a day or two of misery one didn't feel all that sick and I recall a group of us who were well enough to get up and press our noses against the frosted glass behind which the red-haired Sister Greenwood, the only pretty nurse, was thought to be having a bath. So my last term passed happily – too happily perhaps, as my work slipped a bit and I was disappointed, as mentioned earlier, to pass out only third, having been generally top all the way through.

Our last term-end dance went well, assisted by some illegal sherry. A sad note, humorous in retrospect, was struck when

Ollie Round, one of our wilder characters, decided to catch an early train home. Like an escaping prisoner of war, he laid out a dummy in his bed and let himself out of a window. However, his absence was discovered, so on arrival home at Birch Hall, Colchester, he was greeted by his formidable father, Colonel Round, chastised, and sent all the way back to Dartmouth to face (if that is the word) six 'official cuts'. These were administered by cane over a gymnasium box horse by the Commissioned Gunner. Shades of the Old Navy. Ollie then went back home. So that was the last of the Royal Navy College, Dartmouth. It had been tough but fair and towards the end I thrived on it and felt part of the great service for which, in its way, it had tried to train us.

THE RODNEY TERM

My term, the Rodneys, produced no admirals though some of those who were lost in the war would probably have achieved that rank. Ten, or nearly one third, were lost by enemy action. Of those who survived, the highest distinctions were earned after retirement. Duncan Lock, who was passed over for promotion as a lieutenant-commander, became a knight for services to local government. John Somerville was made Companion of the Bath and the British Empire after serving at GCHO Cheltenham, the Government Code and Cypher Centre. I find it of interest – to me – to review the list of the 32 of us who joined in September1931 with their fates, ranks and distinctions to the present (1996).

John BRIDGER	Lost in a submarine in WWII
Charles BRUTON	Dropped a term due to sickness. Retired as a lieutenant in 1946
Michael CHICHESTER	Commander. Signals officer
George CLAYTON-GREENE	Commander (Engineer). Married an American girl. Retired to USA
James COMPTON	Killed in a destroyer in 1940
Alec DENNIS	Commander. DSC. Retired to Canada 1957
Compton DOMVILE	Retired as cadet. Died Canada 1960s.
Ralph DRUMMOND	DSO, DSC. Lost in a submarine
Francis FOWKE	Retired before the war. Served as a Reserve officer. Died after the war.
John GIBBONS	Lt. Commander, Fleet Air Arm, Died
Paddy GILMORE	Commander (Engineer). Died 1980s
Tempest ('Medit') HAY	Captain
Bremer HORNE	DSC, Commander, signals officer. Died 1988
Ian JOHNSTON	Commander. TAS officer
Peter KEITH-WELSH	Captain, signals officer
Hugh KNOLLYS	Lt. Commander. Navigator
Anthony LAWRIE	Killed in Fleet Air Arm 1942
Grenville LIVERSIDGE	Lost in submarines WWII

Duncan LOCK	Lt. Commander. Navigator. Knighted
Norman MACPHERSON	Resigned as Lieutenant, 1946
John MARSHALL	Lost in destroyer *Diamond*, 1941.
Michael MARTIN	Commander (Electrical)
Leycester MAUDE-ROXBY	Resigned pre-war. served as Reserve Lt
Philip MAY	DSC, Lt. Commander, Submarines. Died 1995
George MORRELL	Killed in motor-cycle accident pre-war
David MOTT	DSC, lost in submarines, 1940
Roger NORWOOD	DSC, invalided post-war. Retired to USA
Paul PIERANO	Killed in Fleet Air Arm by Japanese 1942
John PIGOT-MOODIE	Killed in destroyers, WWII
Oliver ROUND	Lost in submarines, WWII
John SOMERVILLE	Resigned as Lt. Commander, 1947, signals officer. CB, CBE, post war
Hugh WILSON	Captain. TAS Officer. Commodore Hong Kong

HOLIDAYS

My holidays were mostly spent at West Kirby with my parents and my brother, with occasional visits to aunts and to Llangollen where my mother's old friend Elaine Richards lived. Years later I married her daughter. My parents didn't come down to visit me at Dartmouth, though there were days when it was possible. It was a long and expensive train ride with a hotel bill at the end, and I don't think they could afford it while they were trying to educate two boys. In fact, the only time my father went away was to visit Uncle John with whom he went on walking tours visiting country churches. They couldn't afford a car and I never saw either of my parents drive one; in India they had a chauffeur. In 1935 when I was 17, I learned to drive on a friend's car and did an alarming test with a woman examiner in the narrow streets of Chester.

My parents were both addicted to betting small amounts on horses, and when my father got a 'double' on Golden Miller for the Grand National and another race, my brother and I each got a bicycle. When we were younger, we used to bicycle sedately round the countryside of the Wirral with my father. We rarely conversed. My brother had by now recovered from his appendix problems and was at King's College Choir School, Cambridge. It was hoped that Alan would become a chorister which meant a marked reduction in fees, but his voice wasn't good enough. However, he got a wonderful education there – a great deal more civilized than prep school. From there in 1936 he went on to Felsted, a public school in Essex which he seems to have enjoyed and where he made many friends. All this must have cost my father a lot of money. Our fees at Dartmouth were paid in full by our parents in those days, as for any public school, and on top of that was the cost of uniforms. So we lived fairly modestly at home, but managed to keep the cook and maid.

I used to play golf with my father and once ventured onto the championship course at Hoylake where we sometimes watched world-famous players like Bobby Jones. I played some tennis and even rugby football, and also remember going otter-hunting with Max Adda and his glamorous wife. We used to drive down to a stretch of the River Severn in a great big car with a monogram on it, a chauffeur and great baskets of food, to spend the day splashing about the river with the otter hounds, occasionally to kill a wretched otter. I still have two of their paws, mounted, to the horror of my grandchildren. Like many country pursuits, in those days there was a purpose to the sport: to keep down the otter population because they ruined the fishing. Nature seemed to be well balanced then, but I doubt if the sport has survived. Max Adda was an Egyptian cotton broker, a delightful and civilized man. Sadly, his wife ran away with the chauffeur, but he remained a dear friend. By chance many years later his second wife, by now widowed, came to live near us in West Vancouver to be near a daughter by a previous marriage. But she didn't stay long.

HMS *FROBISHER*

A new phase of my life started on April 30th, 1935, when I joined the training cruiser HMS *Frobisher* and went to sea for the first time. She was a large cruiser of about 10,000 tons, laid down during the war in 1916 but not completed until 1924 at which time she had few rivals, being equipped with seven 7.5-inch guns and capable of 30 knots. My uncle, old Sir Frederick Tudor, wrote to me and told me that when he was Third Sea Lord, he had the class named for what he called 'Tudor worthies'. So, there were 'Frobisher', 'Effingham', 'Cavendish', 'Hawkins' and 'Raleigh'. One of them was later renamed *Vindictive* after the hero ship of the Zeebrugge raid in 1917. By 1935 she was becoming out-dated, and had been converted to carry a couple of hundred cadets under training.

Here we ex-Dartmouth cadets joined with ex-public-school entries and several young men from Commonwealth countries – Canadians, Australians, New Zealanders and Indians. We also had a group of Chinese. There were three cruises a year, coinciding with normal school terms. We 'Darts' did two of these while the 'Pubs' did three, presumably because we had already had a good deal of naval instruction. Naturally we felt a little superior to begin with, especially as we knew each other well by now. But the Pubs had a broader education and after a while there wasn't much to choose between us. The captain was Piers Kekewich, a fine-looking man with a prominent nose, a ruddy face and a generally distinguished look about him. He usually smoked a pipe with a lot of rather special tobacco overflowing the bowl. He would unbend to have any music-lovers to his cabin in the evenings to listen to records. Commander Amery-Parkes I only remember as a small, rather short-tempered man who turned up early in the morning in ankle-high rubber boots for 'scrub decks'. The other officers seem to have made little impression on me, other than the amiable navigator, Dewar.

Life in a training cruiser has been well described by John Winton in his amusing book *We Joined the Navy*. I actually succeeded in keeping a rudimentary diary during the first cruise. It still embarrasses me to find that I was so irresponsible and flippant. I think that quite a few of us were thus affected after the very tight and restricted life at Dartmouth. Now we could smoke, drink beer and port, and go ashore in strange ports – albeit not very late at night. But it was freedom of a sort. On the other hand, as often happens in life, one moved from being 'top of the heap' in the old school to being a dogsbody in the next. We were well treated but our status was ambivalent. By day one was mainly on a level with the sailors; but in the evening one put on a form of mess undress and had to behave like an officer. I found myself somewhat confused. We actually got paid – a shilling a day – and I wish had kept my first 'King's shilling'; but of course, it got spent at once.

CADET LIFE

Life was a mixture. Some hours were spent at regular classroom instruction in Navigation, Seamanship, Gunnery and so on. Others were spent with the sailors, scrubbing and holystoning decks, polishing brass, stowing hammocks. We got to know them pretty well and a splendid lot they were. I think they found us an amusing breed and looked to fill us up with yarns and tall stories about life at sea. Some of it has only become printable in recent years.

I remember the Marine Corporal of the gangway, with whom I found myself on watch on the quarterdeck, telling me about his runs ashore in Glasgow: 'Christ, I was pissed...' ; the Leading Sick Berth Attendant who loved to describe the treatment for gonorrhoea, the so-called 'hockey stick' in great physical detail, quite a downer; the rather effeminate Signalman: 'Grimshaw... Well 'e used to be lush, but now 'e knows 'e's lush so 'e ain't lush no more.'

Our normal working dress consisted of blue serge trousers, blue sweaters, uniform caps and brown canvas shoes. Some hardy souls chose to go about in bare feet. I tried to do this but soon found myself stubbing my toes on ringbolts and other obstructions, and quickly abandoned the practice. Very few bare footers kept it up for the whole cruise. Another old-style idea was to purchase from naval stores a supply of leaf tobacco. You could buy the leaves, wrap them in spun yarn, perhaps dipped in rum, rolled in the shape of a banana and allowed to mature. It was known as a 'prick'. After a few weeks one cut chunks off with a seaman's knife and smoked them. A lot of trouble for old time's sake. When not under instruction much of the time was spent working 'part of ship'.

There were four parts of the ship for purposes of cleaning: Forecastle, Foretop, Maintop and Quarterdeck. There was rivalry between them. I was a Foretopman and the nub of our competition lay in our 'Fire Queens'. These were hand pumps for putting out fires, rarely used in practice but lovingly polished, painted and gussied up. It was hoped that the captain would pass approving comments as he did his rounds. I must admit that the Maintop Fire Queen outdid ours in splendour. I don't know if it would have functioned. One soon learnt the tricks of avoiding work. Walking round the decks carrying a bucket or other equipment with a purposeful look on one's face soon became boring, and more sophisticated methods were sought. It was particularly desirable to avoid holystoning decks. This involved getting on hands and knees and rubbing the spotless teak deck with the holystone, a brick of sandstone. We would get in a line and proceed backwards until the entire deck in our part of the ship was done and covered in sand. Then it was washed off by a hose wielded by a three-badge sailor (he got the cushy job). After many applications the deck became snowy-white. Such activities made occupation in the old days for the large crews required to man the old-fashioned guns. Now long gone, of course. Another enjoyable activity was 'Paint Ship'. Hanging over the ship's side with two cadets each armed with a paint pot and brush tended towards riotous conduct. But to do it well was quite hard work, resulting in a subsequent 'make and mend', or half-day holiday. Thank goodness we no longer had to Coal Ship as in the old days. We lived in broadside messes: that is, trestle tables running athwartships, on which one rested, fed and wrote.

Occasionally we dressed in mess undress and had a semi-formal dinner followed usually by a concert of ribald songs. I didn't enjoy it much. The previous term of public-school entries had already done one cruise to the West Indies the previous winter. They spared us nothing of the *Tales of Tortola*, banyan picnic parties and a fairly dramatic rescue of a stricken oil tanker called the *Valverda*, of whose name we became heartily sick especially when our predecessors received a share of the salvage money. But this was merely envy. Our forthcoming cruise, though quite interesting, was to be confined to the UK and a few European ports. We slept in hammocks suspended above the mess tables, a new experience and tricky at first. But once inboard one was spared the rolling motion of the ship and felt quite cosy. The use of spreaders at head and feet helped to keep one cool in hot weather with so many at close quarters. It gave us a good idea of the life of a sailor on the messdecks.

SUMMER CRUISE

So, on May 2nd, 1935, two days after joining, we set off to sea. Down the Medway to Sheerness to oil, then off in the evening to Rosyth. Nine years later, I was to take my first command down the same river and on down the Channel. Two days later after an easy passage in a flat calm sea we went under the Forth Bridge. I had spent most of my working hours down in the engine room with the Commander (E), whose 'doggy' I was, trying to trace a leak in a steam pipe. It was very hot, but I avoided holystoning. A week in Rosyth was filled with instruction, team games and visits to Edinburgh where we ate a lot of food and went to the movies. I wandered round the dockyard which was full of semi-derelict V and W class destroyers from the First War. They looked as though they would never go to sea again, but they did, and saved our bacon in the Atlantic only a few years later. Another interesting sight was the famous old liner *Mauretania*, then being scrapped. I went all over the remains of her and found a copy of her deck log on the bridge. It is long gone and the ship has transmigrated into other things. On May 10th we left for Copenhagen after a little trouble on the way out, fouling a buoy and putting a propeller shaft out of action. I was rather scathing in my diary, little knowing that I would bend my own propeller a few years later. The passage across the North Sea found us rolling fairly heavily in an oily swell. I started to feel queasy and went up on deck. There was a full moon and in its eerie light I came across a group of Chinese cadets being sick over the side. They appeared to be a dreadful luminous green colour and made a horrid noise of it. I soon joined them and have suffered somewhat ever since. Next day was calmer and land was sighted in the afternoon. We must have passed over the scene of the Battle of Jutland, only 19 years earlier, though I don't remember any mention of it. Through the Skagerrak, round the Skaw, through the Kattegat and down through the Belts to Copenhagen where we made fast alongside the Langeline, a long jetty close to the city centre.

COPENHAGEN

On entering harbour, a 21-gun salute was fired. I was manning the side immediately under one of the 2-pounder saluting guns which went off with a sharp crack. We wore no ear protection, and very painful it was. So I was rather deaf throughout our stay, and years later this seems to have come home to roost. We spent a week here, and much enjoyed it, this being our first experience of a European city. The crowds were friendly though some criticized the age of our ship, a little hard to take when one looked at their almost non-existent navy headed by an ancient coast vessel called the *Peder Skram* which resembled a flatiron, had been built in 1908 and looked it. [*Peder Skram* was launched in 1904 or 1908 but scuttled by the Danes in 1943 to prevent her use by the Germans. She was nevertheless raised and used as an anti-aircraft ship until Allied bombers sank her in 1945.] There were many pretty girls who were taken over by the sailors when the ship opened to visitors. Also, a raging queer called Harry who caused much hilarity. We cadets were bidden to a *thé-dansant* [tea dance] at the British Legation where there were some even prettier girls. I made some progress with one of them who taught me some Danish, but unfortunately lost her to Ralph Drummond who seems to have had more charm or a better line. We had a busy time ashore, playing soccer, visiting the Tuborg Brewery or spending evenings at the Tivoli Gardens. But our leave expired much too early – 10.30 pm. My one Sunday afternoon's sleep was interrupted when we had to man ship to cheer King Christian as he left harbour in his yacht.

39

I didn't even see him. On May 22nd we left for Oslo, passing Hamlet's castle at Elsinore. A lovely passage up the fjord where the German cruiser *Blücher* was sunk five years later.

OSLO AND TRONDHEIM

Oslo wasn't as much fun as Copenhagen, but the weather got quite hot and I got sunburnt. We played the locals at soccer on a black cinder field, drank beer, sang songs and cemented relations in general. Then, a cruise up the fjords to Trondheim. A lovely trip in windy weather through sheltered waters. Five years later I was to see some of these fjords in less pleasant circumstances but they were still beautiful, snowy, rocky and tree-clad. While at Trondheim three of us went to the railway station to buy return tickets to Hell, a town which lies a few miles up the fjord. Unfortunately, the station was shut so there would be no way back when the time came.

SCAPA AND SCOTLAND

After three days in Trondheim we left for Scapa Flow to find the whole of the Home Fleet at anchor. In later years I was to see a lot more of Scapa than was nice or friendly; mostly in conditions of dark, cold and gales. But this time, close to the summer solstice, it was light for all but a few hours and the weather was kind. I remember one still, light night when the hills were reflected in the water, the air was still, pure and clean and the effect magical. Every day was filled with healthy activities – rifle shooting, general drills, runs, games and instruction. Several of us went ashore for walks and once we rented an ancient car and drove to the very channel where a few years later Gunther Prien took his U47 through to sink the *Royal Oak*. We saw some old blockships from the First War, but it was evident

40

that they no longer blocked the channel and in 1935 there was little or nothing in the way of defences or facilities in what was once again to be the main base in home waters. We left Scapa on June 16th and made our way down the west coast of Scotland, stopping for a day or two at Ballachulish and Campbeltown. Shore activities included walking, climbing and a quick swim in very cold water. On the whole I didn't find the Scottish lochs appealing. On board there was 'engineering' – hours of chipping evaporator coils – studying for seamanship exams, sailing and boxing (not my favourite sport). The captain commented on my whiskers as 'perilously long' and my leave was stopped until they were cut to an acceptable length.

THE 1935 NAVAL REVIEW

Then a passage down the west coast, round Land's End (not seen in the fog), to anchor in Torbay on July 1st. This was a good deal better than Scotland. The weather was hot, the sea reasonably warm, the shops civilized and there were strawberries and cream and beer. I spent one sunny afternoon swimming and got badly burnt. Would I never learn? One evening a ghost from the past – the old *Iron Duke*, Jellicoe's flagship at Jutland, anchored nearby. When I was a boy my Uncle Alick had taken me over another survivor with a splendid history: the battle cruiser *Tiger*. Of course, there were still many officers and men who had served in these. The next days were spent in preparing the ship for the forthcoming Jubilee Naval Review at Spithead [celebrating King George V's 25 years as monarch]. We painted ship, converting her from a handsome light grey to a much duller dark colour, that of the Reserve Fleet. When we sailed on July 10th to join the Squadron, thick fog came and we had an exhilarating time probing through the brume, sounding our siren and listening for those of the other ships which sometimes seemed close and at others a long way off. Before the days of radar, one depended on these rather treacherous sounds as one steamed slowly ahead feeling one's way. Once we nearly plunged into a flotilla of destroyers, identified by sounding their pennant numbers in Morse code. We reached Spithead without mishap and anchored in our allotted place among a large and impressive, though somewhat obsolete, fleet. Nearly all the major warships had been built during the last war and the re-armament consequent upon the rise of Hitler had not yet begun. However, the numbers were impressive and the ships looked superb and in good order. There were several foreign warships, among them a German pocket battleship and the Japanese heavy cruiser *Ashigara*, both of which we were to meet later. The Royal Yacht, the old *Victoria and Albert*, passed between the lines with King George V on board, barely visible to us cadets who manned the rails and cheered to order. The Fleet Air Arm flew past with what it could muster and, in the evening there were fireworks and a display of searchlights which went well barring a few errors. I had to hold a 'port light', a sort of red firework which at first refused to light properly when I struck the match. However, I got it going before anybody noticed.

Next day I got ashore for a couple of hours and went to Alverstoke where my mother was staying with Aunts Beetle and Rose, and we got together with my cousins Helen and Di. A slight cloud passed over the proceedings with the news that another cousin, Mardi, had been in the Quetta earthquake and was believed killed. Later it turned out that she had survived but lost most of her possessions. Next day the entire fleet weighed anchor and went to sea. After a good deal of manoeuvring we formed up in two long lines and the old King was cheered as we went past. It was a windy, sunny day and the whole scene was a memorable one. It was something between the one about which Kipling wrote the 'Recessional' and the later Coronation Review of 1937 when Tommy Woodrooffe distinguished himself with his drunken broadcast 'The Fleet's lit up!' I wonder how many of these ships were still afloat ten years later: *Hood, Repulse, Royal Oak, Courageous, Glorious, Barham,* were sunk, as were the German and Japanese visitors. That evening the 'Mainbrace was spliced' – i.e. there was an extra tot of rum to 'over age'. We, being under 18, got port at dinner to drink the health of Their Majesties, after which there was a lot of rorty singing and horseplay.

BREST AND CHATHAM

The next day we visited the French Navy at Brest. We weren't impressed with some of their older ships but had a good reception at their big new Naval College – a sort of massive Dartmouth in which each cadet had his own study, unlike our old 'gunrooms'. But they were older than we had been. We enjoyed their champagne and biscuits but don't seem to have made any friends. Some of us went on to a cinema and understood about half of it; then more wine and strawberries and a wander around the town. Working hours were filled with examinations at the end of the cruise - Seamanship, Signals and Engineering. I seem to have done quite well and ended up with the maximum accelerated promotion time. Not well deserved, I confess, as I had not been very responsible on the whole. But I wasn't the only one. Then it was back to Chatham at the end of the cruise. There was prizegiving by the C. in C. Admiral Tweedie, the King's Dirk being won by a Canadian, Caldwell. After a lot of hard work, de-storing and cleaning up, we went off on leave until mid-September. I have little recollection of that leave, but remember playing monosyllabic golf with my father and doing some riding.

FINAL CRUISE

In due course, I caught the train south to join again for the final cruise as a cadet. *En route* I met John Marshall who passed on an ugly rumour (alas, proved to be correct) which he had got from the all-knowing and ubiquitous Messrs Gieves, the naval outfitters, that our projected cruise to the Mediterranean had been cancelled because of the Abyssinian crisis with Italy. We were once again to circumnavigate Scotland, a dismal alternative. So, on September 18th we left Sheerness and called, in turn, at Rosyth, Invergordon, Lamlash, Portland and Portsmouth. My diary gave up the ghost early on and I don't remember much of these three months. In September I attended my first naval funeral. A cadet called George Murray had perished 'of mushrooms' and was given the full treatment. We marched for what seemed like miles to the hospital and to the cemetery. Things did not go well. The *feu-de-joie* was ragged and the coffin got somewhat out of control, falling with a crash to the bottom of the grave. We maintained the old naval mien, 'cheerful but subdued', but I regret to report that we thought it was funny. My only memory of Invergordon was of a bike ride to Tain and back, a fair amount of beer and a long free-wheel down the hill at great speed, in the course of which one of our number sailed close to a stout figure who was walking along and tipped his hat off into the gutter. Unfortunately the stout figure turned out to be our cadet gunner, Mr Archer, a formidable figure who to some extent looked after our discipline. After profuse and abject apologies, he was very decent about it. 'I knows you didn't mean to do it', a most Christian view of a silly young person (not me, I hasten to add). He gained our respect. The next port of call, Lamlash, was even more dreary than Invergordon. And but for Mussolini we would have been in the Mediterranean. Maddening. Then there was Portland and Portsmouth which at least had bright lights and girls. The cruise ended back at Chatham on December 9th. So, I finished my four years as a cadet with the accelerated seniority, which was gratifying, though my family seemed to take it as a matter of course. The main thing was the feeling that I had left school at last.

I can't say that I enjoyed the training cruiser much. We were neither one thing nor the other and could have done with a bit more responsibility. But we got a taste of the 'real world' and were beginning to realise that the 'armistice' after the 'Great War' might not last. Hitler had been in power for a year and a half and the German navy was starting to rebuild. Not that I worried about it day by day. Apart from duties and instruction, life was carefree and fun. One had many old friends, the survivors of whom are still friends, as are many of their wives. We lived a great deal to the sound of the wind-up gramophone, and the tunes and lyrics of the day – mostly American – were superb. Cole Porter, Jerome Kern, Rogers and Hart, Irving Berlin, leading to Fats Waller, Count Basie, Duke Ellington, Nat Gonella and others. I could never understand why the older generation thought it 'noise'. Now I'm the older generation and I think rock music is appalling. For recreation, it was mostly strenuous games, meals or movies. Again, we were lucky in our timing with the likes of Astaire and Rogers.

MIDSHIPMAN – HMS *RODNEY*

During the ensuing Christmas leave, spent at home at West Kirby, I received my appointment to the battleship *Rodney*, then lying at Devonport. I joined her in the rain on January 6th, 1936, along with Hugh Knollys and Hugh Wilson of my term. I was one month short of 18 years old, proud of being a midshipman, no longer specifically under training and paid 5 shillings a day. *Rodney* was with some limitations, notably of speed (a maximum of 23 knots) and poor anti-aircraft armament (nothing unusual in those days), a fine ship. She displaced 35,000 tons and had a heavy armament of nine 16-inch guns in three triple turrets, all facing forward. She had a big modern enclosed bridge in a structure known as the 'octopoidal' and was in general roomy and comfortable compared with the older ships. She was the newest battleship in the navy, one of only two of post-war design, having been completed nine years earlier. I remember as a boy seeing her arrive brand new at Spithead. Her sister ship, the *Nelson*, was the Home Fleet Flagship and considerable rivalry existed. We were also part of the Home Fleet, the least exciting of stations. I was envious of some of my contemporaries who were joining cruisers in the Mediterranean, West Indies or South Africa. My turn was to come.

MIDSHIPMAN'S LIFE

We midshipmen inhabited a large gunroom – 29 in all including 9 sub-lieutenants of various kinds. We were presided over by a senior sub., Philip Rhodes, a cool customer that I didn't care for much, He later became a submariner and was lost in the *Salmon* [almost certainly sunk by a mine in July 1940]. There were still remnants of the Old Grand Fleet attitudes towards junior mids ('warts') though there was no longer any bullying. But we had to polish the brass work and perform other menial duties. I have hated brass work ever since. When we arrived on board at Devonport the gunroom was closed so we had supper in the wardroom and an officer was heard to remark: 'What are these things doing here?' Sometime later I was supposed to call the Commander at 0600. I put in for a shake myself at 0530 but never got it. (A likely story, you say, cynically). This, of course, did not suffice and Philip Rhodes said: 'Well, you're damn slack, anyway,' and proceeded to give me six with a sword scabbard. It wasn't much use feeling outraged. However, on the whole I was pretty happy and so was the ship generally. It was quite an eye-opener on how to run a big organisation of 1,500 or so men, effectively. As midshipmen we were required to keep a journal in a handsome volume provided by Their Lordships of the Admiralty. I still have mine and find it a good record of those days, although it was written with a view to weekly inspection by the 'snotty's nurse' [i.e. the officer in charge of the training and well-being of midshipmen] and monthly by the captain, so it doesn't reflect personal affairs as much as Service doings thought fit for senior eyes.

SENIOR OFFICERS

The captain was Wilfred Custance, a rotund and rubicund man who came from a line of distinguished gunnery officers (his father had served with my Uncle John). I later served with his son, known as 'Oafy', the last of the naval line, I believe. We didn't see much of the august person, but I remember his ruddy face peering out of his scuttle as he watched my efforts to bring the picket boat alongside. He was later relieved on promotion to Rear Admiral by William ('Jock') Whitworth who was much later to be my C. in C. and a most distinguished admiral. His son became a great friend but died after the war from leukaemia. In those days the Royal Navy was in many ways a family affair both for many officers and men. The Commander, Alec Madden, also came of a great naval family and went on to be an admiral. So I suppose I started off in the right sort of company. Nearer to my day-to-day experience were the snotty's nurse and my divisional officer. The former, Lt. Commander Baker-Cresswell, the Navigator, later distinguished himself during the war by capturing a U-boat together with its Enigma machine, an important victory although the U-boat sank under tow. He was nice enough, though somewhat remote. The latter, Lt. Commander Paul Voelcker was the senior torpedo officer. He was tall, thin, dry and ascetic. He reminded me of Lieut. Cornelius Vanslyperken of Captain Marryat's *Snarleyyow*. His junior was an abstemious teetotaller called Stileman who bit his knuckles. I remember Voelcker in the wardroom drinking his gin and saying in a deprecating tone, 'And you'll have a lime juice, Stileman.' At the top end of the scale was a remote figure that I rarely set eyes on – Rear Admiral C.G. Ramsay, C.B., sometimes known as 'The Ocean Swell'. All that I remember about him was the fact that his wife was crippled and came on board in a sort of sled pulled up the gangway by a party of sailors rather in the manner of hoisting a boat. They got her going at a fair speed and managed to stop in good time at the top, by skill or luck. Admiral Ramsay was Rear Admiral, 2nd Battle

47

Squadron, which included, in addition to ourselves and the *Nelson*, some old R class battleships from the First World War, unmodernised.

BOAT WORK

When our duties were allocated, I found to my delight that I was to have charge of the First Picket Boat. This meant that I would not normally have to keep watch on deck in harbour, which could be rather a boring occupation, though frantic. My picket boat was about 15 tons, modern, twin screw and diesel-engined. She was a handsome craft, known as the *Queen Mary*. I believe there were only about half a dozen of them in the fleet, all the others being of the old type with single screws, or coal driven with fine bell-topped brass funnels. The diesel boats were cleaner and didn't require 'lighting up' and consequent delay getting underway. Also, the twin screws made them more manoeuvrable coming alongside. In *Rodney* it was, unusually, the practice for the midshipman in charge to handle the engine room telegraphs while the petty officer coxswain steered. The thinking behind this was that it approximated more to the situation which obtained when the captain manoeuvred the ship by orders to the engine room while the actual steering (subject to helm orders) was done by the quartermaster. At first I tended to use a lot of engine movements and was briefly known as the 'Telegraph King' but got the hang of it after a while. It was the greatest fun. Finding one's way around this great ship took a little time.

The upper decks were straightforward but lower down the many spaces and corridors between them were quite complicated and at first it was even hard to know whether one was facing forward or aft, port or starboard. In particular there was a circular walkway around one of the lower parts of 'B' turret known as 'Tattenham Corner' where everything looked the same and there were few exits. Rumour had it that a man had been lost there for days. Fortunately, most of my existence was passed up top. My action station was at the searchlight control on the upper bridge where one could hear and see a great deal. The procedure, which seemed to involve a fair amount of shouting, entailed, first, lighting the searchlight behind the shutters and then opening these to display the searing beam. Woe betide anyone who opened the shutters before the precise moment ordered or failed to get the light going before the exact moment it was to be required. In fact, the light made such an excellent aiming point for the enemy that it wasn't used much in practice.

Another complication which it was important to get right was the system of recognition lights. These were set up on the mast in vertical display in a combination of white, red or green. They were governed by little master tabs which had to be changed exactly at the prescribed times. Their title was V/C V/F. I don't know what it was supposed to stand for, but they were known as 'Very Comic, Very Funny'. In practice the system (a lesson learnt from Jutland) became obsolete in the days of radar (as yet undreamed of). [The Royal Navy first tested radar at sea in 1938].

AROSA BAY AND GIBRALTAR

In mid-January we left the dark and drizzle of Devonport *en route* to Gibraltar. We rolled majestically down the Channel and I felt seasick again, even in this vast ship. However, it wasn't so bad as to prevent me carrying out my duty as midshipman of the middle watch which consisted mainly of making cocoa for the officer of the watch. This was an art in itself as the ship's cocoa was thick and greasy and came in big oblong cakes. One had to shave thin slices off the cake, mix suitably with sugar, pour boiling water in gradually while mixing and topping up with tinned milk. All somewhat nauseating on a heaving stomach. If the result didn't please the officer of the watch it had to be done again. To go with the cocoa there was ship's biscuit, dry as a bone. A short passage brought us to Arosa Bay in the north-west corner of Spain where we anchored fairly far out and I had my first experiences running my picket boat. There wasn't much of interest ashore. The town was small and grubby but a few of us managed to visit, in all innocence, an establishment where some plump ladies danced naked on a table, my first experience of such a performance. While we were at Arosa we heard of the death of King George V and the accession of King Edward VIII for his brief year's reign. Seventy 'minute guns' were fired, something I had never experienced before, nor have I since. A day or two later we sailed for Gibraltar, a place of which I became fond on many later visits. Few share my enthusiasm. From a naval point of view, it was a place to meet old friends, a change from damp England (although the winter could be windy and rainy), and the first taste of the delectable Mediterranean.

RIDING INCIDENT

One day we had a visit from a group of Gordon Highlanders who were stationed on the Rock. I had a bit of luck to be detailed to look after a pretty girl called Daphne Alexander, daughter of a Major in the Gordons. We saw quite a lot of each other after that and used to go riding together around the bay towards Algeciras, in those days quite unspoiled by development and oil refineries. On one occasion we had a lovely supper in a little inn by one of the rivers, and were a bit late to leave. As we were galloping along the beach on the way home, a small child suddenly ran out from behind some bushes and tumbled right under Daphne's pony. We reined in, came back and found the parents creating a scene while the child was yelling its head off. It didn't seem to be injured and I quietened the parents down by leaving my name and ship, and off we went, just in time before the Spaniards closed the gate into Gibraltar. This was lucky because it didn't do to get held in Spanish

50

custody. A duty officer would have to come from the navy to get you out and there would be unpleasantness and possibly a flogging. Anyhow I went off to sea next day. On return a day or two later, a signal arrived requiring Midshipman Dennis to report forthwith to the Vice Admiral, Gibraltar. I put on my best uniform and arrived in some trepidation at the office of Vice Admiral J.M. Pipon. Daphne was already there so it was obvious what it was all about. However, after due interrogation, the great man was nice enough, said that we had done the right thing and that he would send his medical officer to see what damage had been done to the child. In due course we heard that there were no injuries other than bruises and the incident was closed. The only awkward part was that Daphne's mother didn't know she'd gone over the border with me. I was lucky to have a girlfriend on the Rock where they were few and far between. Daphne was great fun and an enterprising girl. She had an all-over tan but sadly I never saw it in its entirety. After we finally left Gibraltar in July, I never saw her again. The Gordons were posted to Singapore and I believe they were still there when the Japanese invaded. I can only hope she got away beforehand. I couldn't find her father in the post-war army list. There was plenty to do in Gibraltar and the climate was good. Years later, Alan read this and, unknown to me, took it upon himself to find out what happened to Daphne. He discovered that she had not gone to Singapore and had survived the war. She married, had children, lived in Scotland but died only a month or so before he would have established contact. It was sad because I would have liked to go over those happy days together.

Tennis, squash, rugby, football and sailing were available and some reasonable meals ashore if you could afford them which I couldn't on my 5 shillings a day plus an allowance from my father who still paid for my uniforms. There were a couple of amusing casinos, one of which boasted an all-girls band, an unusual feature in those days and popular with midshipmen. I climbed the Rock several times, once with a party of sailors on a very hot day. They were in great spirits, as Jack always is when ashore and my lot stuck palm fronds on their shoulders like

51

epaulettes. The hotter it got, the more they joked. My duties consisted almost entirely of running the picket boat; what more could I have asked? At other times we did navigation instruction and were required to take a number of sun and star sights per cruise. And it wasn't easy to fudge one if you failed to get up in time to catch the morning twilight; if you relied on the evening you often found a cloudy sky. Life in the gunroom wasn't too bad, but being the juniors, we seldom got the comfortable armchairs. We could drink beer, port, sherry and wine but not spirits. There was a bit of a library which included a much-thumbed edition of the *Encyclopaedia of Sexual Knowledge*. We still slept in hammocks, though as young officers we were able to employ and pay a hammock boy to lash up and stow. We each had a sea chest in the flat where we slept, and all clothing and possessions had to be kept in that. Food was adequate, provided by a messman and stewards, so we were progressing.

At the end of March, we sailed for England and a leave period, this being the usual routine in the Home Fleet. The only thing worthy of note was passing the German Zeppelin *Hindenburg* on her way across the Atlantic, later to meet a spectacular doom. I have no recollection of what I did on leave which was soon over, and returned to the ship at Devonport. While we were there, Hugh Wilson and I and a couple of others hired a car to drive out to Salcombe to the wreck of the *Herzogin Cecilie*. She was one of the last of the fully rigged 'windjammers', and had run in many of the grain races from Australia. Now she was hard and fast on the rocks and her crew and stores were being lifted up to the cliffs by breeches buoy. She was a sad sight, the last of her era. She never sailed again.

I should, perhaps have mentioned two visits made during our previous stay in Gibraltar. There were three days each at Las Palmas, Gran Canaria and Funchal, Madeira. The former was in those days quite undeveloped and really rather dull. Even the beaches were a bit grubby. We had a friendly party with some locals up in the hills but I had no desire to return. Madeira was more interesting, even then a winter retreat for rich British people. We swam at Reid's Hotel but found the drinks expensive. This time it was back to Gibraltar again, leaving on May 7th, having disembarked Rear Admiral Ramsay because we were due to wear the flag of the C. in C. Home Fleet, Sir Roger Backhouse. The usual flagship, the *Nelson*, our sister and rival, was to refit and the C. in C. would embark on our arrival in Gibraltar, bringing his Staff with him. So, a lot of temporary offices and cabins were built, and we lost our study. Admiral Backhouse was very good to us youngsters and would take us to picnics over to Algeciras in his barge. For some reason several of us were in hospital so the rest of us saw more of him than we normally would. One evening I was bidden to supper followed by attendance at some amateur theatricals in the local theatre. Sitting near the C. in C. in the 'Royal Box', observed by all eyes, I was acutely conscious that I just could <u>not keep my eyes open</u> - late nights in the picket boat and ashore, I suppose. I tried everything I could think of but still kept dozing off and wishing I was elsewhere. If the great man noticed, he didn't say so.

THE LION OF JUDAH

In March 1936, Hitler flaunted the Treaty of Versailles and Locarno Treaties by sending his troops to occupy the demilitarized Rhineland. In doing so, he brutally exposed the Allied lack of resolve to confront Nazi aggression that in turn encouraged a series of other expansionist moves including the absorption of Austria into the German Reich and the invasion of Czechoslovakia in 1938. Appeasement, i.e. making concessions in the face of aggression from Hitler and Mussolini, was the policy of the United Kingdom in dealing with all these problems. Although appeasement was finally abandoned in late 1938, this sequence of international diplomatic events culminated in Britain and France entering the Second War in September 1939, shortly after Hitler invaded Poland. Before this, in October1935, Italian forces invaded Ethiopia and the

British and French Foreign Secretaries Sir Samuel Hoare and Pierre Laval attempted to avoid a broader conflict by allowing Italy to retain two-thirds of Ethiopia. When news of the Hoare-Laval Pact leaked to the press, news of the proposed sell-out caused an uproar leading to Hoare's resignation, although as Alec states below, he was later appointed First Lord of the Admiralty. Their objective was to gain Italian support against German aggression as Mussolini was not then allied with Hitler. Emperor Haile Selassie was forced into exile on the 2 May, arriving at Gibraltar aboard HMS *Capetown* shortly before Alec met him. Haile Selassie's famous speech to the League of Nations in which he criticised the League and the great powers for breaking their promises and failing to come to his country's assistance was made in June 1936.

At the end of May we were honoured by a visit from the deposed Emperor of Abyssinia who came on board to lunch with the admiral. Haile Selassie, Lion of Judah, once called Ras Tafari [Makonnen] and now the Negus [King], was a frail figure, small and immensely dignified. He had brown skin, a black beard, black eyes, black eyebrows and wore a black cloak and a black bowler hat. His cortege drove along the mole; first the outriders on motor bicycles, then a series of limousines carrying the Emperor, Empress and various Rases. Finally there was a very black man on a bicycle, pedalling furiously to keep up with the motorcade. We never discovered his function, but he provided light relief. We did admire Haile Selassie who had just escaped from Abyssinia before the Italians occupied Addis Ababa. Six years or so later we kicked the Italians out and replaced the Emperor on the throne where years later he was strangled by the murderous Colonel Mengistu.[2] I am glad to have seen the Lion of Judah, direct descendant of King Solomon, at close quarters.

LAST DAYS AT GIBRALTAR

A while later there was another sort of 'parade' along the mole. A sailor, very late back from leave, somewhat dishevelled and showing the effects of a surfeit of beer, advanced along the mole seated on a donkey. When the gendarmes rushed down to take him away, he called down to them, 'Have the hounds passed this way, my man?' He probably got off lightly. We spent a fair amount of time at sea, carrying out many exercises, including some full-calibre shoots at battle practice targets towed at high speed by a cruiser. The concussion of these big 16-inch guns was phenomenal, although they didn't hurt the ears as much as the crack of the guns did. At the first salvo my cap flew off and I hit my chin on the gyro compass from which I was taking bearings. I have thought since of the difficulty of thinking clearly in action when such a cataclysmal racket is going on all the time. It is so easy for historians to criticise decisions taken under such conditions. One thinks particularly of Beatty and his opponents at Jutland. In between spells at sea we lay at the South Mole, at the inner end as befitted the Fleet Flagship. But I still ran the picket boat across to Flagstaff steps or the Depot ship *Cormorant* to cut short the walk ashore. Some time was spent rehearsing for the King's birthday parade which took place in June. We felt the lack of the Gordons who were sent off to Palestine (eventually to Singapore) to deal with the Arab-Jew troubles which were violent even in those days when each side had the British to blow up. The parade went well enough except that we wore those white helmets known as 'solar bowlers'. Quite a number of them blew off as we rounded the end of the Rock and ran into a strong crosswind. The march was also made tricky by the presence of a regiment of light infantry who marched at a much faster pace but had to maintain the same speed over the ground.

Only one other incident in the *Rodney* sticks in my memory. I used to attend communion service once a month in the ship's chapel, which had to be shared among religious denominations.

One morning I was rather late in attending, to find the only available seat was right in front. After a short while it became apparent that something was wrong. Little bells were ringing, incense was being swung and the congregation kept bobbing up and down. Being right in front I had no one to follow so clapped my hand to my mouth, tried to look sick and beat a hasty retreat. I think I had hit the R.C. day. In the middle of July most of the Home Fleet ships left Gibraltar for home. Now the war in Abyssinia was over, the tension with Italy eased somewhat, though only for a short while. We left for an uneventful trip back to Devonport and I went off home on a couple of weeks leave. Just before we went, Hugh Wilson and I were appointed to HMS *Enchantress*, the Admiralty Yacht, for the period of the First Lord's cruise to the Mediterranean.

ADMIRALTY YACHT

The reason for this diplomatic tour of Malta, Cyprus, and the Greek Corinth Canal was to inspect the defences of local British naval bases and show support to smaller countries vulnerable to fascist aggression during the Spanish Civil War. Predictably, this British action was interpreted by fascist-Rome-based *Giornale D'Italia* as an aggressive move towards Italy.[3] Later in the year, Germany and Italy signed the first of a series of treaties establishing the Rome Berlin Axis and a closer relationship between them although it was not yet a formal military alliance. Subsequent British and French diplomatic efforts culminated in the Anglo-Italian Agreements of 1938 intended to prevent the Axis becoming a formal military alliance between Italy and Nazi Germany. However, in ignoring the earlier Italian occupation of Ethiopia and confining its provisions to maintaining the existing order within the Mediterranean it merely perpetuated the system of appeasement soon to be exposed as a sham.

This was splendid news, especially as I wasn't much enamoured of battleship life, well run though the *Rodney* had been. The new appointment, though likely to be a short one, promised to be interesting and good for one's career. So, while on leave I had to provide myself with new uniforms for which my father paid. Almost on the day we went on leave, and no sooner than the Abyssinian crisis had passed, a new and perhaps more sinister one arose. The Spanish Civil War started – in some ways a preview of World War II – evoking passionate feelings on both sides in many countries, including my own. Hugh and I joined the *Enchantress* in Chatham on August 10th. She was a new sloop originally armed with four 4.7-inch guns and designed as an anti-submarine escort. Her two after-guns had been removed to make accommodation for the Board of Admiralty. This included some handsome cabins, a reading room and a fine dining room. A year or two later when Duff Cooper became First Lord, he had yet another box-like structure built, in which he could do correspondence and write his books. It was known as the 'Duff Coop'. So, the ship was a kind of hermaphrodite, a fine modern warship in front and what is nowadays invariably called a 'luxury yacht' aft. She was the successor of that famous *Enchantress* in which Winston Churchill spent so much time when he was First Lord before the First World War. Even in the 1930s there were such remains of the spacious Victorian and Edwardian days. *Enchantress* really looked a picture. She had a black hull whose enamel finish was kept polished. Just above the waterline was a white line with the usual red anti-fouling paint below it. The upperworks were white, the funnel and masts a handsome primrose yellow. The decks were spotless white teak and the crew wore rubber shoes for silence. She displaced about 1,200 tons with a crew of 125.

There were normally only six officers, we two midshipmen being specially lent for the cruise. The captain was Commander R.F. Jolly, a 'cool customer' in my view, who always wore yellow wash-leather gloves when he went about the ship. He was pleasant enough though rather remote to us youngsters. It was his fate early in the coming war to be fatally wounded on the bridge of the destroyer *Mohawk* when she was attacked by German bombers in the Firth of Forth. He refused to go below and continued to con the ship until he collapsed and died. He was posthumously awarded the Empire Gallantry Medal, later converted to the George Cross. [The EGM was superseded by the George Cross on 24 September 1940 with existing recipients exchanging their insignia for the new award.] The first-lieutenant, Jock Hayes, was efficient as one would expect and had a great liking for malt whisky which he drank in moderation. There was a qualified navigator as No.2, called Meares, a famous name in that trade. The sub-lieutenant, the Hon. David Chubb, was an amiable fellow, as were the 'Chief', Bird, and the Gunner, Banks. Hugh and I shared a small cabin with a bit of a squeeze. We each had a bunk instead of a hammock. My main duty was as navigator's assistant which I greatly enjoyed. Otherwise we were mainly employed as watchkeepers in harbour, where it was busy.

We left Portsmouth on August 15th for Gibraltar. The weather was pretty fair but there was an oily swell and I very soon felt sick and was virtually useless for a couple of days. I had more or less got used to the motion of the great *Rodney* but this was my first small ship and I began to wonder whether this was the life for me. This damned seasickness was to plague me all my seagoing career. It wasn't much help to know that Nelson suffered too. However, I recovered after a while and enjoyed a few drills and *en route* we passed the *Graf Zeppelin* on her way to South America. A pretty sight with no future. We also passed a very dirty Spanish destroyer called the *Churruca* after a Trafalgar admiral, I believe. [This was Cosme Damián de Churruca y Elorza, who died heroically commanding the ship of the line *San Juan Nepomuceno* at Trafalgar.] She was on the so-called 'Government', or Communist, side in the civil war which was now raging. After a short stay in Gibraltar we sailed for Villefranche where we were to pick up the First Lord and party. Passing Ivica [Ibiza] three corpses were seen in the water, the first signs of warfare. On the 22nd we anchored in

Villefranche bay and very attractive it looked. There were the usual salutes and exchanges of calls. My journal notes that the British consul told us that the French navy was 'rotten with communism'. They were certainly anti-British, never having forgotten Trafalgar; though the destroyer anchored nearby was friendly enough. I had my first look at Nice and Monte Carlo and did some surfboarding behind the fast motor boat – these were the days before water-skis. We also had some enjoyable sailing races won by Hugh Wilson who was and is a superb helmsman.

SIR SAMUEL HOARE AND PARTY

On the 26th we embarked the First Lord and his party. This consisted of Sir Samuel Hoare himself; his wife Lady Maud; Lady Worsley, a friend of hers, along for the cruise; the Naval Secretary, Rear Admiral G.C. Royle; the Private Secretary of the Admiralty, H.V. Markham, whose familiar signature appeared on all admiralty fleet orders (A.F.O.s); the Parliamentary Secretary, William Waldorf Astor; and the flag lieutenant to the board, Lieutenant Commander 'Tommy' Thompson. Some of these are worthy of note, many years later. Samuel Hoare was of course a well-known politician about much has been written. He was sometimes called 'Slippery Sam'. He was one of the older men later blamed for appeasement of the dictators. He had recently lost his job as Foreign Secretary after the national revulsion against the 'Hoare-Laval' pact designed to satisfy Mussolini and bring the Abyssinian war to an end. Hoare's association with Laval, who was executed after the war for collaboration with the Nazis, did not improve his reputation. But he bounced back and was now First Lord of the Admiralty. He appeared to me to be as smooth as silk, a politician to his toenails which were encased in elegant 'co-respondent' shoes [a type of low-heeled brogue shoe with two contrasting colours]. H.V. Markham was one of the very top civil servants who ran

59

the navy. Shades of 'Pinafore'! He told me that he had been one of the examination board before whom I had appeared for entry to Dartmouth. W.W. Astor was in his twenties and a very nice fellow whom I got to know a little bit doing de-cyphering work together. Many years later as Lord Astor he got badly tangled up in the Profumo scandal with Christine Keeler, Mandy Rice-Davies, the Soviet naval attaché and all. He never really recovered from it and died young. Lieutenant Commander Tommy Thompson went on to become Winston Churchill's personal flag lieutenant and is to be seen in many of the group photographs of the Great Ones like Roosevelt and Stalin. Some memoirs have accused T.T. of pushing himself to the front, or near it, on these occasions. We thought him 'plausible'.

THE CRUISE

That afternoon we sailed for Malta, passing through the Straits of Bonifacio between Corsica and Sardinia where perhaps my great-grandfather had sailed with Napoleon[4]. One evening I was bidden to dine in the saloon with the First Lord and his party. I remember that the conversation turned to the *Graf Zeppelin* which we had sighted en route to Gibraltar. Sir Sam held forth about airships and said that when he was Minister for Air, he had pressed for their adoption by Britain as a long-range bomber force. Admittedly he was talking about the mid-1920s; but I recall thinking what a stupid idea it was. I held my tongue, of course. The dinner went well and they were very nice to me, especially Markham, the P.S. Next day we arrived in the Grand Harbour, Malta, the first of many visits for me. There were only three capital ships in harbour at the time, due in part to the need for keeping an eye on the Spanish civil war. But the *Queen Elizabeth, Repulse* and *Glorious* looked very fine at their head and stern buoys. Our days there were filled with salutes, bugles, and comings and goings by senior officers of all sorts, so Hugh and I were kept busy on deck and at the gangway. It was all very ceremonial. We had been escorted into harbour by the *Grenville*, then brand new and fated to be sunk in our company when I was in the *Griffin*. I managed to get some bathing and to visit my old friend Antony Lawrie in the cruiser *London*, moored nearby. Then we were off to Famagusta in Cyprus to meet the First Lord again, he having sailed in the 'Q.E.' for exercises *en route*.

I believe the official purpose of his visit was to inspect the possibility of establishing a base there as Malta was so vulnerable and close to Sicily. But the harbour was much too small and the Greek and Turkish population none too stable, which is still the case today. A walk around the splendid fortifications and a few lovely bathes were about all I could manage before we were off again, for the fact that the island belonged to Italy didn't seem to bother anyone. [Actually it was British.] In those days we treated the Aegean as our own. We hung around Phaleron Bay [Greece] waiting for a friend of Lady Maude's but no one showed up so after a tantalising distant view of the Parthenon we set off through the canal. Straight and narrow, with steep sides on either hand, it was an interesting, short and enjoyable trip until we headed out into a fresh gale in the Gulf of Corinth which made for an uncomfortable passage to Malta.

By now I had more or less got my sea legs and was able to function but I was thankful to get into the Grand Harbour. After a day or two there we were off to Gibraltar and home. The only incident of interest happened because of some more rough weather west of Malta. We were proceeding rather slowly with the sea on the quarter and rolling a lot. Complaints arrived on the bridge from the First Lord's quarters. It happened that about that time we got in the lee of some land and the rolling was much abated. Sir Samuel and more particularly Lady Maud were convinced that the captain could well have reduced the discomfort earlier if he had thought about it. So there was some coolness for a while. VIPs can be tricky and so can the Mediterranean. Our onward passage to Portsmouth was calm and pleasant as we went close in to the Portuguese coast to see what might be seen – mainly fishing boats. But thick fog came down near the Isle of Wight, our gyro compass failed and we had to anchor off Yarmouth with the tide behind us, and came close to parting our cable when fortunately it held and we were able to arrive in Portsmouth harbour in time. Here the party disembarked and went off to London by train.

It was September 22nd. It was while we were lying alongside the South Railway Jetty that I met another distinguished personage. I happened to be on deck when the august figure of a full admiral appeared on the dockside, strolling along with a walking stick. It was the Commander-in-Chief, Portsmouth, Sir William Wordsworth Fisher, already almost a legendary admiral who had recently been C in C, Mediterranean. While ashore in Malta he used to ride about in an open white Rolls Royce like a big galley on wheels. He was a personality of the old school, known as 'The Great Agrippa'. Had we gone to war with the Italians in his day he would have made his name. He and the whole fleet had been ready and willing to fight, but London quailed at the idea, so we didn't close the Suez Canal which would probably have finished Mussolini before long. As it was, W.W.F. kept the fleet's morale on the very top line. As an example of his touch, it was said that in Gibraltar at the big meeting after the combined fleet manoeuvres he had summoned the gun layers of the 15-inch turrets of all his battleships present – perhaps about thirty men. To the assembled ship's companies, he pointed out this small group alone might hold in their trigger fingers the fate of the British Empire. Hyperbole, perhaps, but with a grain of truth, especially in the mid-1930s before the battleship became eclipsed by the aircraft carrier. It was this somewhat frightening figure that stepped up on our gangway to be met by myself and a hastily summoned first lieutenant. We walked around the upper deck and the Board's accommodation with him and all went well until he stopped in the saloon opposite a chart showing our recent itinerary. The great man stuck his forefinger onto a spot on the coast of Cyprus. 'What happened there?' he demanded. We racked our brains but couldn't come up with anything more significant than the First Lord going ashore. 'Weren't you aware

62

of any history?' came the voice from on high. 'Saint Paul landed there!' Sadly, it wasn't long before Sir W.W.F. died prematurely. Had he lived, he might well have been First Sea Lord in the coming war in place of Sir Dudley Pound. I can't help feeling that he would have been a match for Churchill's bullying.

LAST DAYS IN THE YACHT

I managed to get off for weekend leave, to be greeted on our return by our new appointments to HMS *Resolution,* an old battleship now being brought out of reserve. This was not welcome news as neither of us wanted another battleship. However, we were told that this was only to be temporary, and were unofficially offered China as our next choice, which we accepted with alacrity. After some haggling about dates we were to join the *Resolution* on October 10th and so stayed in the *Enchantress* for passage to Chatham, but were robbed of the next cruise to Scotland. At Chatham the First Lord reappeared without his ladies and there was much high-priced visiting. I remember Commodore Jack Tovey, later Admiral of the Fleet, who only eight years later in this same port let me take command of the *Savage.* A great man. There was also a final dinner party in the saloon, attended by the full Board of Admiralty, headed by Lord Chatfield who had been Beatty's flag captain at Jutland. There were also other distinguished admirals whom I am glad to have met – Dunbar-Nasmith, Henderson and Noble. Our time in the yacht was climaxed by a dance which went well. My journal remarks that one of the ladies slipped on a ladder and broke one of her high heels. The quartermaster and I had to choose between sawing the other short to match, or replacing the missing piece with a matching chock. We chose the latter course of action. Next day Hugh and I set off for Portsmouth to join the Rolling Reso.

INTERLUDE IN THE *RESOLUTION*

The Spanish Civil War that Alec mentioned earlier broke out in July 1936 when Franco and other Spanish Nationalist generals led a rebellion against the Republican government. Franco received help from Germany (including the notorious Condor Legion), Italy and Portugal with France and Russia assisting the Republicans. Thousands of UK volunteers went to fight, but the British government remained neutral. Royal Navy warships including *Resolution* were sent to enforce an arms embargo made under the Merchant Shipping (Carriage of Munitions to Spain) Act 1936 on the combatants. The war dragged on until April 1939.

I am sorry to say that I found her a sad come-down from our beautiful yacht, and even the nine-year-old *Rodney*. She was already nearly twenty years old, a veteran of the First World War and not modernized since, apart from the addition of two large anti-torpedo bulges which further reduced her already inadequate speed. But these bulges may have saved her when she was torpedoed by a submarine off Dakar in 1940. She had originally been designed as a coal-burner but had been switched to oil before completion. She was a real relic of the Grand Fleet. Her eight 15-inch guns were still a formidable armament but lacked modern control. She had one experimental anti-aircraft gun which frequently jammed. As for accommodation and other facilities she was just as dated. Our midshipman's quarters were well below decks: the bathrooms were actually below the waterline and various valves had to be manipulated in the right order or you risked a flooding, a nearly capital offence. When we joined her, she was away at the north end of Portsmouth dockyard near the coal stacks. She had been in reserve for some time and there was coal dust everywhere. Now she was to be brought to full complement and sent to hang around the Spanish Civil War area.

The officers made very little impression on me, and I only remember a few of them. The captain was Sir Lionel Sturdee, Bart, son of the well-known admiral, Doveton Sturdee who won the battle of the Falkland Islands in 1914, sinking the *Scharnhorst* and the *Gneisenau*. [In effect, Sturdee wiped out the German East Asia Squadron as a fighting unit.] Sir Lionel gave an impression of gloom only lightened by a highly polished brass plate over the door to his cabin. It read: 'KEEP SMILING'. I saw quite a lot of him as one of my duties at action stations was to be his 'doggie', i.e. messenger and general factotum. My instructions were to keep out of the way but to be instantly available. I had been unaware that the ship bore such a distinguished name. Captain Cook had commanded her namesake 160 years earlier on his second voyage around the world, with George Vancouver as one of his officers. I was attached to the Torpedo division. As the ship had no torpedoes, the main duties of the men were electrical and didn't lend themselves to noisy drills such as the gunnery department delighted in. In fact, taking advantage of a lapse in organization I managed to miss most divisions and parades. I responded rather subjectively to leadership, or the lack of it. Perhaps I still do. The Commander was called 'Batchy' Bayne for good reason.

After a week or so of harbour drills, we sailed for Tenerife in the Canary Islands to look after the King's interests and those of his loyal subjects during the civil war. *En route* we formed landing and boarding parties to be ready in case of trouble. After doing a full power trial which achieved about 20 knots into a head sea, we arrived at Santa Cruz de Tenerife on October 26th to relieve the Cruiser *Leander*. The island was peaceful, having been taken over by General Franco's 'Insurgents'. Red and yellow flags were flying in place of the red, yellow and mauve. Large numbers of people of all ages were in uniform of one kind or another, and the evenings saw many of them walking along the Malecon with girls on their arms. It was here that Franco had started his coup which overthrew the left-wing government in Madrid and started the bitter and bloody civil which lasted years. Naturally nearly all the people we met were staunchly for Franco. Anyhow nobody dared admit otherwise. But if half the stories of corruption, strikes and brutality under the Government were true, one could understand the relief of the bourgeoisie when the military and church seized power. There were gruesome stories of the treatment of the priests and nuns by the rabble in the days before the coup. It was strange to hear the opposite story when we got back to England where the majority seem to have supported the left wing. I was lucky again to find myself running a picket boat rather than watchkeeping in harbour. These boats were quite different from *Rodney's*. They were steam driven instead of diesel, with lovely polished brass funnels which flared out at the top. With one large propeller instead of two, the boat was much trickier to handle especially when coming alongside port side to as the kick when going astern was quite substantial and had to be allowed for by giving her a neat swing in the opposite direction at the last moment[5]. Quite a good turn of speed could be achieved if the stoker piled on the steam, especially, like a horse, on the last trip home.

SCHLESWIG-HOLSTEIN

About a week after our arrival, an old German battleship used as a cadet's training ship anchored nearby. She was the *Schleswig-Holstein,* built in 1907 and a veteran of the battle of Jutland when she had been hit by a British shell. The spot had been converted into a sort of chapel and was lovingly tended, full of mementoes and portraits. In 1936 the Germans had just started to rebuild their navy with formidable ships like the *Scharnhorst,* but until recently had only been allowed to keep a few old crocks like the *Schleswig-Holstein,* used for training. In the event, she fired some of the first shots of the coming war when she was used to bombard the Polish port of Gdynia. We got along well, as always, with our German opposite numbers, dined in each other's messes and sang appropriate songs. We were always to find them more congenial than the French, and although even then the German nation had a reputation for ruthlessness and brutality, the Germans seemed so far to be 'gentlemen'. I wonder how many of our friends survived the war, especially those who went into U-boats.

CANARY ISLANDS

Next day we left for Las Palmas, carrying out gunnery practices on the way. I had been there before and hadn't much cared for it. This time we went alongside the mole so it was easier to get ashore. The Hughs and I were invited to a party where the local Spaniards were celebrating the imminent capture of Madrid. In the event, this did not happen for many months but we had a jolly evening of singing and dancing. Then it was back to Santa Cruz and more practices and drills. Some of these seemed to be rather obsolete, like getting out the kedge anchor, involving a lot of lifting and lowering. Seamanship has been described as 'an obsolete method of lifting heavy weights'. It all required good organization and team work, and errors could be dangerous to life and limb. The anchors and cables of these great battleships were enormously heavy and cumbersome, as were the big wires needed to move things around. The next brief visits were to Orotava – banana trees everywhere – and Santa Cruz de Palma. Then back to Tenerife and Las Palmas for our last week or so. On November 8th we sailed for home leaving the Canary Isles at peace in the hands of the victorious fascists. The weather was cloudy and rough, making it hard to complete the requisite number of navigational sights.

SHEERNESS AND CHATHAM AGAIN

We reached Sheerness on December 5th in bitterly cold weather, a strong tide with the wind against it. After the balmy days in the Canaries I felt the cold quite severely, though normally it didn't bother me. My first agreeable surprise was an appointment to the cruiser *Suffolk*, then refitting but about to recommission for service on the China station. This was good news indeed, as a Home Fleet battleship was a dreary life. China promised to be fascinating and a cruiser much more agreeable. Hugh Wilson and Hugh Knollys were to come with me.

ANTI-GAS INTERLUDE

While awaiting our new appointments and Christmas leave, we went for a week to the R.N. Barracks at Chatham for an 'anti-gas' course. Gas warfare was much on people's minds in those days, after the horrible experiences of the soldiers in the trenches of the last war. It was generally expected that in spite of treaties such barbarian attacks would be repeated, and on civilians as well. The course opened with some gruesome pictures of men badly disfigured by bullets and shell splinters, the message being: 'is gas warfare any more inhumane than this?' Once accustomed to the idea, we went over types of gas known at the time, their effects and methods of protection and decontamination. Regrettably my old gas mask, whose container was rusted beyond repair, was considered for exhibition in the Gas School museum as an example of how not to look after one's respirator. We also lost marks for fooling around in the decontamination exercises, and slapping white paste around like the Marx brothers. However, the final exam was dead easy and we all passed. Then home to West Kirby and a week's leave.

THE ABDICATION

During this time the abdication of King Edward VIII took place. Rumour and gossip filled the newspapers and general conversation. I sympathised with the King whom I had last seen playing the drums at our term-end dance at Dartmouth. But Wally Simpson was unacceptable to most of us. Prime Minister Baldwin seemed to come out of it well but on the issue of rearmament he let us down badly at a time which was becoming more dangerous by the month.

HMS *SUFFOLK*

I was highly delighted with my appointment to the *Suffolk* and the China station. Indeed, the next year was one of the happiest and most interesting of my life. The two Hughs and I joined her at Chatham on January 6th, 1937. I was to be the senior midshipman in a gunroom of nine plus the sub-lieutenant, Bobby Elsworth, Sub-Lieutenant (E) John Sedgwick and Paymaster Sub-Lieutenant Leslie Sutherland who was later lost in the destroyer *Exmouth* in 1940. We got along very well. At the top of the scale, the captain was H.C. Phillips, a vice-admiral. He seemed to me to be an ideal leader, quiet and decisive, ruling with a firm velvet glove. Towards the end of my time he was relieved by C.S. Sandford whose claim to fame, I didn't realise it at the time, was that he was one of the only three survivors of the battle-cruiser *Invincible* when she blew up at Jutland in 1916. The Commander was Sam Smith, a splendid administrator, easy to work for. Likewise, the wardroom was a harmonious lot of whom I particularly remember E.E. (Nutty) Penton, the navigator and snotty's nurse, an imperturbable pipe-smoking philosopher who unaccountably never got promoted, but remained a friend to many, including Hugh Knollys who kept in touch with him when he died many years later. Then there was 'Duggi' Tait, a tall red-faced lieutenant-commander who later distinguished himself as an escort commander in the Battle of the Atlantic, but perished in a U-boat battle in which his ship was torpedoed after being immobilized when she rammed a U-boat. [Thought to be Commander Arthur Andre Tait, captain of HMS *Harvester* who died shortly after the depth charging and ramming of U444 in the North Atlantic on 11 March 1943.] An unusual character was Conrad Rawnsley, a lieutenant who was full of ideas, though perhaps not too well fitted for the peace-time navy. He resigned and became an expert on antiques[6].

All in all, she was a happy and proud ship, an example of how a medium sized ship should be run. She was one of that big class of 10,000-ton 'County' class cruisers with eight 8-inch guns, designed primarily for trade protection in the great oceans. She was therefore given a high freeboard, almost like a huge yacht, most roomy and comfortable, and able to keep the seas for long periods of time. Her main armament, after some teething troubles, became most efficient and she had been modernized to some extent to carry eight 4-inch anti-aircraft guns and more short-range weapons. She had just been fitted with a big ugly square hangar which carried two amphibious Walrus aircraft with another perched on a transversely mounted catapult. To compensate for all this, she had some of her quarterdeck cut down a deck which reduced her accommodation somewhat though she still remained a most commodious habitat for both officers and men. Although somewhat open to criticism compared with her American and Japanese counterparts, this class of ship did very well in the war, serving in all theatres under all conditions. The class of thirteen (including two Australians) lost only three. Two in the Indian ocean in 1942 to Japanese aircraft carriers while quite unsupported, and the *Canberra* in night battles in the Solomon Islands. *Suffolk* herself survived a massive air attack from Stavanger in April, 1940, and I remember seeing her limping into Scapa Flow with her cut-down quarterdeck nearly awash. She made her name by locating the *Bismarck* in 1941.

When we joined her, she was lying in Chatham dockyard having completed a major modernization. I found, once again to my delight, that I was to have a boat to run. This was a motor boat fitted with a 'kitchen rudder', a new device which consisted of two halves which rotated around the propeller. By altering the direction and position these two halves faced, one could move the boat forward, backward or even sideways, to some extent. Control was affected by a wheel attached to the steering wheel, and it took some getting used to; but once mastered it was easy to manoeuvre the boat under almost any conditions. After a few days we dropped down to Sheerness where it was wet, cold and windy as usual, and I went on several runs in the strong tides to try and master the boat. Then we left for Portsmouth, doing a full power trial on the way – marred somewhat by a hot bearing which reduced us to 27 knots on one engine.

FAST BOAT TO CHINA

After ammunitioning and other last rites, we left Portsmouth for China on February 9th, 1937. Then it was the 'all-red' route to Hong Kong: Gibraltar, Port Said, Aden, Colombo, Singapore. At each of these places the Union Flag waved; a remarkable state of affairs which would only last a few years. At Gibraltar we saw the German pocket-battleship *Deutschland* which had just bombarded Almeria after a Spanish Government 'plane' had attacked her. The civil war was still raging and we painted red, white and blue stripes on B turret so that there should be no mistake. Malta was full of the Mediterranean fleet and very smart they looked. From then on, all the ports were unfamiliar territory to me, increasingly exotic and exciting. In those days before mass travel they were visited by only a limited number of people. At Port Said we disembarked a small pack of foxhounds destined for the army in Palestine who were trying to establish a hunt on English lines. What the Arabs and Jews (some of whom were hunting them) thought about it, I can't imagine. The Red

71

Sea was relatively cool but at Aden it was hot enough to shift into tropical rig: white shirts and shorts. I have often thought that grown men look silly in shorts, other than sports, and that officers, at least, should wear long trousers, as do the Americans. Minicoy in the Laccadives – first sight of a coconut palm; Colombo in sticky heat. A memorable evening at Mount Lavinia swimming in phosphorescent sea, carrying a packet of cigarettes on my head to the raft. A magical introduction to the tropics under those brilliant stars – not a worry in the world. Years later when I took my wife there, the beach was dirty and the hotel food covered in flies. I think Ceylon was a better place under the Raj – for most. The Malacca Straits, flat oily calm, and a mishap.

MISHAP

The catapult with which our Walrus amphibians were launched ran athwartships with a slight extension on either end which was run out when one of these aircraft was to be fired off. On this occasion the Walrus was sitting nicely on its trestle revving up its engine. The order was given to launch but instead of shooting off at an increased velocity, the trestle with the Walrus on it merely progressed slowly along the track. The pilot, Spike O'Sullivan, at first increased his revs to a maximum, and then, realising what was happening, cut them right back and started to bale out. The aircraft reached the end of the track and then toppled slowly into the sea. Spike got out pretty quickly, followed by the Telegraphist Air Gunner, but it took a while for the observer, a plump lieutenant called Tarver, to appear in a large bubble. Luckily injuries were only minor, though of course we lost one of our three aircraft. These Walruses were extraordinary looking beasts, sometimes known as Shagbats, driven by a pusher propeller and only capable of rather low air speeds. They needed a bit of a chop to bounce them off the water. They were recovered after landing on the water by taxying

72

up to the ship which usually made a calm downwind. The observer then busied himself by hooking onto a hook lowered by the ship's crane. Clumsy though they were, they did provide the ship with 'eyes' for a good many miles in its trade protection role. They could take off and land on sea or land, and could carry a golf team complete with clubs.

HONG KONG

On then to Singapore for a brief stop and at last our destination, Hong Kong. The port of those days bore little resemblance to the metropolis of today. To me it was exciting, exotic, strange and fascinating. It was only thirty years since the death of the Dowager Empress of China, the Republic, and the abolition of the mandarins and the old regime. The harbour was full of junks and sampans, none of them motorised as yet. The tide of mass tourism had not touched it. Kai Tak airport was then a grass strip and the main hotel was the low-level Hong Kong Hotel, known for some reason as the 'Grips'. The ferries to and from Kowloon were as busy as they are today and the landing places were always full of hawkers and little boys selling everything from notches to paper snakes on sticks. There was the ubiquitous smell. There were nearly always foreign warships present, which meant that at colours every morning, the national anthem of every ship in the harbour must be played before the Godsave, all of which could take a very long time.

All over China the 'chit' system prevailed. This meant that you could sign for almost anything and didn't need to carry lot of cash. A sort of preview of today's credit card, on the honour system. The bill would come to the ship in due course and of course one always paid up. The trust shown on both sides says something for the reputation of the imperialists, at least for honesty. When we had commissioned at Chatham, we already had on board a nucleus of Chinese cooks, messmen and stewards, and very clean, willing and cheerful they were. I still

73

remember Tai Hui (sometimes teased for f...ing himself silly when ashore), and Ah King our gunroom steward – long-suffering and good tempered always: 'Yessir, I go fetch'. We still spoke some of the old pidgin English which now seems to have vanished.

Within a week two of our arrival in Hong Kong a horde of male relatives of the nucleus crew arrived on board. They were never obtrusive or in the way and did a lot of work not only for the cooks and stewards but also for our sailors. One would meet a huge tray coming up a ladder with underneath it a tiny 'Cheeseye' Chinese boy holding it above his head. Goodness knows they made very little money but it was better than starvation which was the lot of many mainland Chinese in those days. There were also sampans with crews of women who kept our ship's side in order. After the Japanese had started to get really nasty a few months later, ships were all required to muster at short notice and count the number of unofficial Chinese on board. I forget our actual figure, but it was rather startling as a proportion of the real crew. There is no record of any spying or sabotage, and these supernumeraries became just as proud of the ship and its performance at regattas and so forth as the regulars.

A few miles along the coast at Mirs Bay and Bias Bay piracy was still flourishing. The pirates would board coasting vessels as ordinary passengers, then take over the bridge and engine rooms under arms, take the ship into a remote creek, loot it, hold some passengers for ransom or torture or both, and sink or abandon her. Many of the coasters had barbed wire entanglements round the bridge and engine room hatches to keep the pirates at bay. Some of our naval ships would keep an anti-piracy patrol in these bays and go to the assistance of threatened ships. This was a symptom of the general lawlessness and misery which prevailed on the mainland. For twenty or more years, China had been plagued by independent warlords who assembled armies, took over areas, looted and plundered and retired in comfort and safety to Singapore or Hong Kong. By 1937 the forces of Chiang Kai Shek had gradually obtained mastery over much of the country, other than the communist strongholds. They were corrupt too but did represent the country as a whole, flew a distinctive 'gear-wheel' flag and boasted a navy of obsolete cruisers and gunboats.

For us, life ashore was fun with lots of exercise; golf at Fan Ling, riding, and sailing. On five shillings a day one could do quite a lot. When we arrived at the end of March it was by no means hot but already humid with a blanket of cloud over the Peak. Our first month was spent mainly in working-up exercises and drills, in and out of harbour. My action station was a relatively responsible one as Rate Officer in the gunnery control tower. Armed with a pair of binoculars my job was to estimate the 'inclination', or direction in which the enemy was going. This, passed down by telephone to the transmitting station, governed the ranges sent to the guns and was a vital part of our ability to hit or straddle the target and to keep on doing so. Sometimes it wasn't easy to see whether the enemy was going slightly towards or away from our line of fire, but there were various clues, and one got quite good at it.

PUTO SHAN

Early in May, we left Hong Kong on a cruise northward, the first visit being to Puto Shan in the Chusan archipelago at the mouth of the Yangtze Kiang river. It had been warm in Hong Kong but we ran into thick fog off the islands and soon shifted into blue uniforms. Puto was a fascinating place. It was in fact a holy island full of Buddhist temples and shrines and rarely visited by Europeans. There were no cars and it felt untouched by modern developments. I later discovered that the British had attacked occupied Chusan in the early 1840s during the 'opium wars'. I have a copy of the 'Cree Journals' [*Cree Journals: Voyages of E.H. Cree, Surgeon R.N., as Related in his Private Journals, 1837-56*] in which a naval surgeon made excellent watercolour sketches of the scenery and actions. It hadn't changed much in a hundred years. I managed a long afternoon ashore and wandered around. There were fearsome gilded statues, strange carved animals and an overpowering smell of joss-sticks. The pilgrims, many of them would be carried from shrine to shrine in litters, get out, light joss-sticks and move on to the next. The Goddess of Mercy, Kwan Yin, inhabited this island which was consequently free of snakes and dangerous animals. We heard that there were still tigers on Chusan. I spent a happy afternoon taking photographs. A clammy, cold fog came down when we got to the jetty so, not feeling like waiting for the ship's boat, we chartered a sampan and wended our way under sail and oar towards the ringing bell of the ship at anchor. A memorable day.

NANKING

Then off to Nanking to be there for the coronation celebration of King George VI. After a tricky night passage through the islands of the Chusan archipelago, we arrived off Woosung early in the morning and embarked a pilot for the passage up the Yangtze. This took a full day, Nanking being situated nearly 200 miles up from Woosung, counting the many curves and bends. I spent a fair amount of time on the bridge watching the pilot who seemed to know the channels perfectly without a glance at the chart. As they varied all the time, this was quite a feat. The river was wide at the mouth, narrowing gradually between low, flat muddy banks without many towns or villages. The main interest lay in the river traffic – junks of a type quite different from those at Hong Kong; low and flat with square sails. Then there were the great log booms on which whole families lived in little shacks for the passage down the river. There were also numerous sampans, customs vessels, merchant ships and the occasional naval vessel for which we had to be alert to pay and receive the proper acknowledgment by bugle, and sometimes saluting gun.

After anchoring for the night above Chinkiang we arrived off Nanking in the morning to find several foreign naval ships and much of the Chinese fleet. My boat was busy taking officers of the guard hither and yon. The muddy water flowed strongly downstream, so we all wore lifebelts, it being highly dangerous to fall in. With the wind against the tide there could be a nasty swell. The ship had to weigh anchor every few days so that it didn't get covered with a heavy layer of mud and be past recovery. May 12th was Coronation day, filled with salutes, Church parties and receptions. All manner of ambassadors and officials came on board and there was a strong smell of moth balls as the various uniforms and feathered hats came out of boxes. One dignitary was seen to be wearing a mourning band, doubtless last worn for the funeral of King George V, removed by his wife as he was about to board a boat. Ships of several navies were present: USS *Augusta,* flagship of Admiral Yarnell, a Japanese destroyer, and many Chinese ships. The Italian gunboat had moved quietly away so as not to take part in the celebrations. There was a ball ashore at the embassy in the evening and some of the girls we met there came down to Shanghai to see us again.

There was, I was told, a party at a lower level on board one of our gunboats, the *Cricket,* at which a diplomat's cocked hat was filled with goldfish. She and the *Gnat,* also present, I was to meet again in the Mediterranean under somewhat different circumstances. The day ended with a firework display and all in all it was a memorable one, probably the last of its kind in China. While we were at Nanking, I had a couple of good days ashore on horseback, riding in the country outside the city's ancient tombs and past the immense memorial to Sun Yat Sen. The city itself was a sad place, much diminished from its great days and shrunken within its ancient walls as though it was an old man with clothes too big for him. The ravages of many war lords had destroyed much in the last twenty years. Worse was to come at the hands of the Japanese only a few months later. Eventually the capital was to return to Peking where it had been before the revolution. My other happy day was spent shooting snipe in the reeds on the opposite side of the river. We tramped through great reeds of high bamboo-like grass, then an area of low muddy sedge. There were plenty of birds about to begin with, but they were hard to reach and even harder to hit. But we did have some success and returned to the ship muddy, wet and cold but satisfied. After all the celebrations the ship weighed, turned and went down the river to Woosung and then up the much smaller Whangpoo river to Shanghai.

SHANGHAI

This was an experience indeed and I was glad to have experienced what was nearly the last of the old scene dominated by the Europeans, Americans and Japanese. Much has been written about Shanghai, and as this is only a narrative I shan't make much attempt to describe it. I found it to be a place full of wonders. The modern bund, where lay the club with the longest bar in the world, contrasted with the age-old sampans and junks being loaded by poor skinny coolies. The smell of drains, the 'foo-foo' barges carrying night soil to some unknown destination down the river; the constant spitting of the Chinese on the jetties – one waited after the throat-clearing for the actual hawking which came sometime later; the chanting of the labourers; the clatter of the trams; the lights at night, neon signs in Chinese which were the more beautiful for being incomprehensible. Freedom to go where we wished ashore, subject to limited means. The Russian so-called 'princesses' in the night clubs (Lucy 'Chaircover' springs to mind); the western clubs with all sporting facilities; and the local European girls, some of whom had followed us down from Nanking along with their parents.

I ran my boat every other day until late at night, and on days off went ashore as soon as possible and stayed up late. One evening, well after my leave should have been up, I chanced to arrive at the same time as Captain Phillips. I told him truthfully that I had been escorting a young lady home. 'Good,' he said and that was that. One night we were up all night but had taken riding clothes ashore and went for an early morning ride with our girl friends to return on board looking virtuous and fit but very short of rest. And one memorable night I won the jackpot on a fruit machine in a night spot (the only time in my life) and even so had to sign for the taxi back to the jetty. The International Settlement was a remarkable place with its own police and law, where the Europeans lived a separate life surrounded by hordes of Chinese. They must have resented the situation deeply but most were glad of the money and employment which the westerners brought.

SUMMER IN WEI HAI WEI

Since 1865, the China Station's area of responsibility comprised the coast of China and its rivers, the sea around the Dutch East Indies and the western Pacific Ocean. Although *Suffolk* was relatively modern, the fleet mostly comprised older light cruisers and destroyers with China's navigable rivers patrolled by flat-bottomed gunboats such as the Insect–class *Gnat*. As Alec recounts below, *Suffolk* visited the fleet's bases in Singapore, Hong Kong, and Weihaiwei (Port Edward), known today as Wehihai. Port Edward was a pleasant summer posting, providing 'a welcome refuge from the equally hot, but extremely humid, climate of Hong Kong, to the south.' That the British fleet was here at all stemmed from fears of Russian expansion into the area during the late nineteenth century, but it remained in place to protect British trade interests in China's waterways, especially the long and winding Yangtze River. Other western nations did the same.

Various day and night exercises were carried out on passage, which soon blew away the cobwebs. Wei Hai Wei was in some ways the farthest-flung outpost of the Empire. It was a rocky island, only four or five miles round, situated just north of the tip of the Shantung peninsular. Between the island and the mainland was a capacious sheltered anchorage which could accommodate the whole of the China Fleet, and more, in safety. Britain had a ninety-nine-year lease on the island which was used as a summer base for the fleet. It was far healthier in summer than Hong Kong, and although it got quite hot by day there was usually a fresh breeze and the air was dry and invigorating. Over the thirty-odd years of our occupation the navy had established some good sporting facilities – football grounds, tennis courts and a golf course. There were handsome sick quarters presided over by a surgeon commander who was the only officer to stay there all year round. There was a small hotel with a 'Missy Annex' where those wives who were rich enough to follow the fleet (there weren't many) could stay. There were some simple repair facilities employing Chinese carpenters and artisans. I shall always associate with Wei Hai the smell of pine needles in the sun. It was a lovely place.

We swam a lot though the water was cool, and played golf using the charming Chinese boys as caddies. In the clubhouse after the game were long, cool John Collinses, another taste I associate with those days. Of course, we were kept very busy as this was the time of year for all sorts of exercises, practices, drills and inspections. It was also the venue for the fleet regatta on which a great deal of store was set. To win on points and be 'Cock of the Fleet' gave immense kudos. So, for some time beforehand, crews were made up, boats were sandpapered to cut down the weight of paint, bottoms were hardened and muscles developed. I rather hated it. The boats were heavy as were the oars and there was really as much brawn as skill involved. A lot depended on morale and by this time *Suffolk* was clearly a happy and well-run ship, and we were determined to win. As, indeed we did under the ship's mascot 'Albert', the Suffolk Punch, a great big model horse which was hidden in the aircraft hangar until the day. Also kept under wraps was a huge 'Cock' which of course was only revealed when we were declared the winners. What would have happened to him had we lost I can't imagine. There was a lot of betting by all comers, including our Chinese hangers-on. Another memorable day.

DESTROYER TIME – HMS *DIANA*

On July 2nd, Hugh Knollys, Hugh Wilson and I were transferred to the *Diana* for our destroyer time which was supposed to be two months but actually lasted more than three due to the Japanese attack on China which started on July 7th. This altered the whole routine of the China fleet and incidentally put an end to any hope of a cruise to Tokyo which would have suited me because my cousin Sir Robert (Leslie) Craigie was Ambassador. *Diana* was my first experience of destroyers, in which I was to spend most of my career at sea. She was actually not a very good example. The captain, Lt. Commander J. (Jackie) Machin, was a lean, figure sardonic figure who didn't see eye to eye with his First Lieutenant, R.M. (Willie) Sandbach, a dark short-tempered fellow who used to ride horses at Happy Valley in Hong Kong, competing with the little Chinese jockeys and, as we thought, up to all their crooked ways. The result was an unhappy and not very efficient ship. The No. 2 was Adrian Northey, an amiable phlegmatic and efficient officer who kept things calm in the wardroom. There was also the Sub-Lieutenant, Pooley, who didn't make much impression, the Chief and Gunner (T) whose names I forget, and an amusing, worldly and congenial Commissioned Supply Officer, 'Sloppy Stuart', with whom we midshipmen got along well. *Diana* was typical of the inter-war destroyers; about 1,350 tons, four 4.7-inch guns and eight torpedo tubes. A good design but lacking in any effective anti-aircraft armament. This must have alarmed our later Captain (D), Hickling, a man known as 'High

Angie Hick' who was to be, quite rightly, obsessed with the coming menace from the air.

Being midshipman, I was lucky to get the captain's sea cabin when in harbour and later the sick bay when not occupied, so I lived in comparative luxury while the Hughs shared a double cabin. A few days after we joined, the captain asked us whether we drank gin. 'Oh no, sir, we're not allowed to until we're 21.' 'Well, in this ship, you're 21 today.' And so, we started to drink gin. The idea was that we should help to shoulder the burden of entertaining the numerous 'taipans' [usually a European-born businessman running a Hong Kong trading house] who found their way on board in the various small ports we were to visit. I believe they thought that, like them, we had an expense account. We did not, and this hospitality came out of our own pockets. But it was sometimes repaid ashore. Midshipmen were paid five shillings a day, but gin wasn't more than twopence a glass. To begin with I hated it. We had no ice or cooling apparatus and the little pony glasses would appear on a large tray with a choice of lukewarm water, angostura or lime to dilute the tots. 'Boy, bring a cloud of gin,' was often Jackie Machin's cry when we had such guests on board. To begin with I used to flip as much as I could with my finger, not being used to spirits nearly neat. However, in due course I learned first to tolerate, then quite to like it, especially when long and cool. Poor Jackie Machin never got the *Diana* going successfully and I believe never had another destroyer command [Alec was unaware that Machin commanded the K-class destroyer *Kelvin* from October 1939 to June 1940]. In 1941 he perished when the battle-cruiser *Hood* was sunk by the *Bismarck*. I remembered the lesson years later when I was afflicted with an inefficient first-lieutenant.

Meanwhile we were kept pretty well up to the mark and expected to know every inch of the ship and what every nut, bolt, valve, pipe and vent was for. It was certainly excellent experience, and in ways one learnt a lot from an unhappy ship in contrast to the happy one we had just left. An example: Lying in Tsingtao a few days later, the first lieutenant had stopped the midshipmen's leave for some reason, now forgotten. We were in the wardroom when the captain came in looking for someone to go ashore with. He paid no attention to our protestations so off we went. We all went to some night spots, and only returned on board at dawn to be met by an angry Willie Sandbach, who was even more infuriated when we pointed out that we had gone ashore at the captain's 'orders'.

CAPTAIN (D)'S INSPECTION

Our first Captain (D) was R.S. Benson. He took an uncomfortably close interest in the midshipmen, starting with having us individually to (but not, as we feared, for) breakfast with him. This was an old naval practice. Conversation was limited as for much of the time he was behind the *South China Mail* or some other paper. He certainly got to know our names and faces, so at his inspection he required one of us to be at hand at all times and was liable to fire all sorts of questions at you. You had to keep cool and never prevaricate. The inspection, on which our C.O.'s promotion tended to hang, went badly. The torpedoes didn't get off when they should due to a slip-up in the drill so we had to go around again. Various other things went wrong and the final analysis reflected rather poorly on the ship. Preparing for this occupied much of July, although we got ashore for swimming, golf and tennis quite a lot and I got to love the island which was called Liu Kung Tao. On re-reading my journal which was admittedly written for the eyes off my seniors, I find it remarkable how busy we were with exercises, drills and practices.

THE JAPANESE INVASION OF CHINA

This summer cruise of 1937 took place against a background of increasing tension with Japan, a former British ally. Sadly, on American insistence, the Anglo-Japanese alliance that endured throughout the First World War ended when the USA made it clear to Britain that continuing this arrangement would only damage future Anglo-American relations and hinder negotiations for the Washington Naval Treaty finally signed in 1922. The resentment felt by the Japanese from this rejection was a major factor in the breakdown of international relations leading to war with America, Britain, the British Empire and the Dutch Empire in 1941. With the Second Sino-Japanese war breaking out from July 1937, the wider outlook for world peace deteriorated still further and the atrocities carried out in Nanking (The Rape of Nanking), only recently visited by *Suffolk*, became the worst and most infamous example of Japanese wartime cruelty. Over a period of six weeks the Japanese committed countless atrocities including the murder of up to 300,000 civilians.[8] As Alec observed below, local relations between westerners and the Japanese in China were tense, but apart from the few well-publicised incidents he mentioned, such as the machine-gunning of British ambassador Hugh Knatchbull-Hugessen's car by a Japanese fighter plane near Shanghai on 26 August 1937 and the bombing of the USS *Panay*, most found themselves left alone. The Panay Incident occurred on 12 December 1937 when Japanese naval aircraft bombed and strafed an American gunboat sinking her, killing three men and wounding many others. During this incident, HMS *Ladybird* was shelled with many casualties but remained afloat. The Japanese eventually apologised and paid compensation but insisted American flags were not visible and the sinking was a mistake. It is generally believed to have been an unauthorised action rather than a mistake and the incident undoubtedly hardened American opinion against Japan.[9] It is often argued with justification that the Second Sino-Japanese war marked the real beginning of the Second World War as it merged with the other conflicts and continued until the Japanese surrender in 1945.

But the progress of the war started to make itself felt and thereafter we were to spend most of our time along the China coast, protecting the interests of his Majesty's subjects. The normal routine of North in summer and South in winter came to an end. The fleet sailed on August 3rd to their various destinations. We set off for Tsingtao which was not very far away, but on the way we ran into some very nasty weather. A typhoon was approaching. At first the sea was flat calm but as we rounded the end of the Shantung peninsular we could see a merchant ship labouring in a heavy swell. Once around the corner we ran into it ourselves. Soon afterwards the wind got up and we spent a most unpleasant night wallowing southward. We studied the books about typhoon behaviour, starting with that sultry but indefinable feeling that all is not well, and bearing in mind that if you face the wind, the centre of the storm should be 120 degrees on your right hand. I felt seasick again. All exercises were cancelled and we arrived off Tsingtao next morning, prepared to ride out the storm in its spacious harbour and also to see what the Japanese-Chinese situation meant for our nationals of whom there were many in the city.

TSINGTAO

Tsingtao was a most interesting place. It had been seized by the Germans in 1898 as part of their 'place in the sun'. It would be fairer to say that it had been leased to them for 100 years, much as Wei Hai Wei and the New Territories of Hong Kong had been leased to us by the treaties of that time when China was weak. The Germans had made an unmistakeable mark. The buildings were Teutonic, the city clean and well run, surrounded on the landward side by heavy fortifications on and around the main hills called 'Bismarck', 'Moltke' and 'Iltis'. The cupolas and guns, though much damaged, were still to be seen. In 1914, the Japanese, nominally on our side in WWI, though in practice looking after number one, had besieged and captured it but had to their disgust to return it to China after the war. Now they were about to capture it again. In the bay lay some Japanese cruisers and some of their most modern and forbidding looking destroyers, much larger and more powerful than ours and painted a dismal dark grey with their names in white in Japanese script. As yet they had not landed, but the town was in a state of tension awaiting them and many Chinese were moving fitfully in and out of town. There were also some American ships present with whom we made friends as always.

We spent about ten days anchored off Tsingtao waiting for a typhoon to come our way and for a Japanese landing. Although the wind got up and we set anchor watch, the typhoon passed to seaward. Japanese cruisers and destroyers came and went, but nothing happened and we gave some leave after the wind abated. One evening we received a signal from shore to say that one of our less reliable sailors, A.B. McDonough, under the influence of drink, had started to swim off to the ship. We and the USS *Canopus* shone searchlights on the sea which was quite rough, and it was felt that he had little chance of survival. However, eventually a sodden figure was seen in the beam of light. He was hauled on board and later punished, but much admired.

Alec Dennis, Royal Naval College, Dartmouth. (Dennis family album)

HMS Frobisher in the Firth of Forth.
(Imperial War Museum. Crown Copyright expired)

HMS Suffolk, Shanghai 1937. (Dennis family album)

Royal Yacht Enchantress at Malta. (Dennis family album)

Monk at Puto Shan. (Dennis family album)

Buddhist Temple, Puto Shan. (Dennis family album)

Cock of the Fleet. (Dennis family album)

HMS Diana at Tsingtao. (Dennis family album)

Lt Commander Machin, Shanghai.
(Dennis family album)

German fort
at Tsingtao.
(Dennis family
album)

Bomb damage,
Yangste river.
(Dennis family
album)

Bomb damage, Nanking. (Dennis family album)

Bomb damage, Nanking. (Dennis family album)

Chinese village. (Dennis family album)

Aircraft wreckage from Hong Kong typhoon. (Dennis family album)

Hong Kong and Kowloon. (Dennis family album)

Hugh Knollys relaxing. (Dennis family album)

Fishing boats on the Yangtse. (Dennis family album)

Burning waterfront. (Dennis family album)

A Supermarine Walrus aircraft aboard HMS Rodney, 1940. (Coote, R G G (Lt), Royal Navy official photographer, Imperial War Museum, Crown Copyright expired)

Rifle range, Port Edward. (Dennis family album)

From left, Jack Fenn-Clark, Jon Walley & Alec Dennis. (Dennis family album)

John Lee-Barber, October 1940. (Dennis family album)

Crew of *Griffin*. Front row centre: John Lee-Barber with Jamie.
Back row fourth from left: Alec Dennis. Back row centre (tallest person): Jon Walley.
Front row right: Jack Fenn-Clark. (Courtesy of Sarah Lee-Barber and Roger Harrison)

October 1940. West of Gibraltar Straits

Johnny and Sue's wedding in Alexandria, 1939.
(Courtesy of Sarah Lee-Barber and Roger Harrison)

Admiral Sir Hugh Binney, when Governor of Tasmania, 1948.
(Archives Office of Tasmania. Copyright expired)

HMS Opportune at Plymouth, 1944.
(Hampton, J A (Lt), Royal Navy official photographer. Imperial War Museum.
Crown Copyright expired)

Front left: John Kennard. Third from right: John Lee-Barber.
(Courtesy of Caroline Kennard. Kennard family album)

Scharnhorst in harbour, 1939.
(Public Domain. US Naval Historical Center)

Admiral Sir Bruce Fraser, 8 May 1943.
(Mason, H A (Lt), Royal Navy official photographer, Imperial War Museum.
Crown Copyright expired)

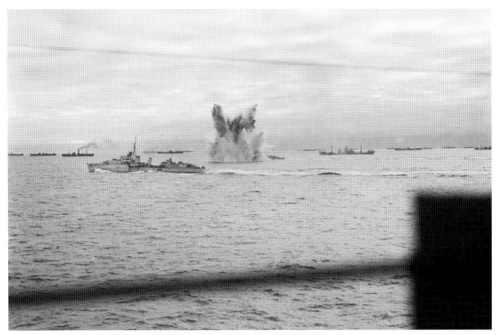

Convoy PQ18. An underwater explosion close to HMS Ashanti with HMS Eskimo in
the foreground. (British Newsreel Pictures. Crown Copyright expired)

CHEFOO

After a day at sea attending on the aircraft carrier *Eagle* who was exercising with her pathetic complement of eighteen Swordfish biplanes, we were sent off to Chefoo, not far northwest of Wei Hai Wei. We stayed there for a couple of weeks until the end of August. Chefoo was the American northern base, corresponding to ours at Wei Hai Wei; much more of a town but not nearly so attractive a place. On the other hand, the Americans had provided, as usual, lavish facilities for their sailors ashore which were put at our disposal with their usual generosity. We made good friends with some of their four-stacker destroyers, played softball with them and tried to introduce them to cricket. We found them highly amusing. On one occasion one of their rather unwieldy old destroyers came alongside with a crash, bending or snapping a series of awning stanchions. Her skipper was profuse in his apologies. 'Gee, captain, I rang the backin' bells, but she wouldn't back.' On another day when we plied them with unaccustomed gin in our wardroom, their captain eventually rose to his feet saying to his first lieutenant, 'C'mon Shorty, get on your horse' – and fell flat on his face and had to be put to bed in one of our cabins for a while. In return we watched excellent movies.

We midshipmen also spent some time ashore with some of their ensigns who had enough money to rent a flat in the town where we played cards and drank 'hot wine'. As we were all much in the same boat in China, we became quite close and used each other's facilities whenever necessary. It was reminiscent of the American admiral's famous remark many years earlier in China: 'Blood is thicker than water' [a much-quoted remark by US Commodore Josiah Tattnall to justify his support for the Royal Navy in the Second Opium War of 1856-60 against the Qing dynasty of China]. As in Tsingtao, the situation was tense and there were many refugees in northern ports, though it was only a matter of time before the Japanese occupied the whole coast. But as Chefoo and Wei Hai Wei were to some extent Western bases they had remained technically Chinese but free from occupation – so far.

It was while we were there that the Japanese made themselves exceedingly unpleasant up the Yangtze by bombing the USS *Panay* and machine gunning the British Ambassador Knatchbull-Hugessen. During our time in Chefoo, I visited a home for orphans, run by nuns. In it were rows of very small Chinese girls, busy sewing patterns with the most minute stitches. It was said their eyesight was permanently damaged – but the alternative was probably starvation as many of them had been sold or abandoned by their parents. Life was cheap and girls of no account.

SHANGHAI AND THE SOUTH

At the beginning of September, we made a short visit to Wei Hai Wei where we had our Captain (D)'s inspection. Then we left for Shanghai, stopping to pick up a passenger and mail at Woosung. The passage up the Whangpoo river was fascinating. All along the river were anchored Japanese destroyers which were busy bombarding Chinese positions ashore. As we passed, the usual courtesies were afforded by bugle or pipe, the gun's crews turned towards us and grinned and then went on with their bombardment. A lot of damage was to be seen to buildings including a tall factory chimney with a hole right through the middle of it. Japanese aircraft hovered around with their red roundels later to become such a menace. They came, I believe, from aircraft carriers out to sea, which we saw. There wasn't much danger to us except for the odd Chinese reply, but we put on tin hats and I for one felt uncomfortable and a bit foolish in mine.

When we reached the Bund [waterfront], there were a few signs of damage, notably to the Cathay Hotel where a Chinese bomb had landed and killed many people. It had been intended for the Japanese flagship *Idzumo*, a very old cruiser which was moored in mid-stream. Sadly we were not to stay in Shanghai which I never saw again. Instead we were sent off to Foochow to relieve the *Delight*. Actually, we had to anchor in the Min river below Pagoda Anchorage and opposite Sharp Peak Island where there was little to interest or amuse. The Chinese had blocked the river further up so that one could only reach Foochow by boat, and our only person to get there was Willie Sandbach, the First Lieutenant. However, some off the well-known lacquer merchants came down in sampans and we were able to get some lovely things at low prices. I wished I had more than five shillings a day to play with.

There were three English families on Sharp Peak Island, all middle aged except for one very plump daughter with whom we played some tennis on their makeshift court. Otherwise there was nothing to do but walk and visit our old friends of the USS *Barker*, watch her movies and give them gin in return. We had laid in large quantities of beer for the sailors, and tried to keep them amused with all sorts of games of skill and chance. Meanwhile we had to watch out for floating mines and await developments. I remember a lovely old Chinese man who appeared in a sampan and produced a 'service certificate' listing ships of the Royal Navy which he had visited and supplied, going back many years. We duly filled in the space for our current visit. I heard later that when the Japanese eventually occupied Foochow and the Min river, he and many like him who were 'friends of the British' were beheaded. We midshipmen were kept busy studying and completing reports of destroyer construction electrical layout. I was quite glad when we were relieved by the *Dainty* (Commander R.M. Dick, who later had a distinguished career as S.O. Chief of Staff to Admiral Cunningham) [Royer Mylius Dick became Staff Officer (Plans) & Deputy Chief of Staff, Mediterranean Station]. We left for Hong Kong passing some Japanese cruisers and destroyers which were lying off the mouth of the river. They had a trick of exchanging identities and, having established ours, replied with unintelligible letters.

THE HONG KONG TYPHOON

On arrival in Hong Kong we saw some of the devastation caused by the recent typhoon. Some eighteen ships were blown ashore including a 20,000-ton Japanese liner, the *Asama Maru*. There was much speculation about what was to be done with her. One school of thought suggested that she should be converted *in situ* into a gambling and gin palace. I believe she was eventually got off. There was much damage to houses and thousands of Chinese who lived afloat lost their lives. The *Suffolk* had been lying in harbour at a buoy and had to steam so as not to drag the moorings. In the middle of the night a Chinese merchant ship drifted out of control, hit the *Suffolk*'s bows, careered off into the dark and turmoil and ended up lying half over the coast road. *Suffolk* lost her Walrus flying boat off the catapult and had to be docked to replace her bow plates. I was sorry to have missed the fun. She was now repaired and away at Amoy so we had to spend a further spell in *Diana* until we could catch up with her.

SWATOW

We were only five days in Hong Kong before sailing for Swatow where we arrived on September 30th to relieve the *Daring* (Commander Barnard, who became one of ABC's staff officers during the war, and was later my admiral in Washington, U.S.A.) [Vice-Admiral Sir Geoffrey Barnard KCB, CBE, DSO & bar was appointed Naval Attaché to the Joint Services Commission, Washington, DC, in 1954]. Swatow was rather an unprepossessing port situated on a muddy, reedy river. The Chinese town had the reputation of being full of anti-westerners, but there was a more salubrious area across the bay where the western taipans lived. Those gentlemen, who must have been bored with each other's company, tended to arrive on board

H.M. ships at an inappropriate hour such as 1030, expecting to be filled with gin (duty free but at our expense). They were one and all, especially the consul, worried about the Japanese threat. This of course was the reason we were there and they seemed to feel that they owned us which was ironic because they paid no British income tax whereas we did. However, they could be fun and interesting to talk to, and I became fairly expert in disposing of my gin without actually drinking much of it.

After a late lunch the captain would sleep under the awning above X gun, on some elegant pale blue sheets; then go ashore if conditions were suitable. We couldn't walk ashore because of the hostile feelings of the natives, but there was a Western Club for meals (officers), and a certain amount of tennis and football. There was an American ship present which had been there for two months and were heartily sick of the place. She was the USS *Asheville*, an ancient and impressive craft. At this time the U.S.A. had barely got into rearmament at all. The U.S. Navy was all white except for stewards who were all black or Filipino.

I was amused in one wardroom when their captain rang the bell, a hatch flew up and a big black face appeared and said: 'Did you buzz me, Boss?' An interesting local manufacture was pewter. I bought a beer mug with a glass bottom and had my name inscribed on it in Chinese. It usually raises a smile from any Chinese who reads it and I wonder what it says. Our stay was not very comfortable because there was another typhoon warning, so we left moorings which were too close to a lot of merchant ships, and anchored up the bay. It rained and blew hard and we spent some time at anchor watch but eventually the storm passed out to sea. We also expected air raids, of which there had been a few, but nothing happened during our stay.

Our time in both Swatow and *Diana* came to an end on Chinese National Day, the double tenth. The C. in C. China, Admiral Sir Charles Little (though malicious tongues said it was really Lady Little) arrived off the port in the flagship, the *Cumberland*, en route from Shanghai to Hong Kong, stopping for a look at the ports on the way. *Cumberland* was too big to enter the harbour so *Diana* went out to pick up the great man while Hugh Knollys and Hugh Wilson were delivered to the flagship for passage to Hong Kong to re-join *Suffolk* at last. The only jarring note was that we were to do a destroyer exam shortly after arrival.

Just before we left Swatow, there was an incident typical of life afloat in China. There was a sort of mutiny on board one of the British coastal steamers with the Chinese crew threatening the officers. Our Sub., Pooley, was sent over to restore order, armed with a walking stick and a party of sailors. The threat was enough and all turned out well, without violence. The trip to Hong Kong was a short one. It was good to be back in the dear old *Suffolk*. She had just arrived from Amoy where everybody seems to have bought Amoy Cats – a local product made of papier-mâché with a head which swung back and forth in a realistic fashion. Very appealing and cost practically nothing. I would have liked one but it wouldn't have lasted long. Our arrival in Hong Kong coincided with that of the crew of the cruiser *Capetown* which had been a long way up the Yangtze when the Chinese blocked the passage below her. As she was stuck up in Hangkow for the duration, this body of sailors was sent down by train across China. They had an eventful passage which included the gratuitous bombing of the railway track by the Japs. I have an interesting book about their adventures, part of a general description of the 'Sino-Japanese incident'.

Almost at once we three found ourselves doing the Destroyer exam. It turned out to be easy, particularly as one of the examiners had to leave unexpectedly early because his transport left for England in the afternoon instead of the evening. We were barely a week back in the *Suffolk* when it was decided that our Air Course must be squeezed in before we were due to sail for Wei Hai Wei. Accordingly, we presented ourselves on board the Aircraft Carrier *Eagle* which had just arrived.

She was an old vessel, having been converted in 1924 from a battleship originally built for Chile before WWI. So she was large but only carried eighteen aircraft, a pathetic outfit compared with the Japanese carriers of that time. The course, though short, was the greatest fun. Designed, I'm sure, to tempt young officers into the Fleet Air Arm, it nearly succeeded in getting me to volunteer. I can't remember why I did not except that the F.A.A. was still in the hands of the Royal Air Force and had a low priority for men and material. The Navy at last got control of their own Air in 1938, [fully in 1939] too late to be effective in the imminent war. So it never really recovered and I doubt if I would have survived the war as a pilot or observer. Anyhow, I loved flying in these strange 'stringbags' (Swordfishes); with their open cockpits you really felt you were in the air. We did some dive bombing and my ears hurt abominably until I got used to it. But my happiest memory, that I retain clearly to this day, was flying over Hong Kong at night, over the water past the lights of Victoria which, though nothing to what they were to become, were magical to see. It was a night of full moon and we came so low that I felt we were dodging the junks. It was lovely. *Eagle* was in harbour much of this time so we were landed at Kai Tak airstrip which was then only a grassy dusty strip. It was to be worked on by prisoners of war to start the new runways, which have grown to such enormous size. It was much nicer then. We had a couple of days at sea and were looking forward to deck landings, but the weather turned nasty, the ship started pitching, and landing became tricky especially as the pilots were out of practice. So we weren't taken up, an omission I regretted as I never had another chance to land on a deck.

We returned to the *Suffolk* the evening before she sailed for Wei Hai Wei. This was not normally the time of year to go up there, but a cruiser was needed in the north to keep an eye on the Japanese. So, we were to spend the whole winter at Weihai or Tsingtao.

WINTER IN NORTH CHINA

Wei Hai Wei in autumn and winter had quite a different feel. For most of our stay we were the only ship present, in contrast to the main part of the fleet when we were last there. The island of Liu Kung Tao was a few miles off the mainland of the Shantung peninsular where the actual little town of Wei Hai Wei lay. The only shore establishment manned in the winter was the R.N. Sick Quarters where Surgeon Commander Shaw lived in solitary state. His daughter Jean had been much in demand when the fleet was in, being a pretty girl of exactly the right age for young officers. We saw quite a lot of her this time and eventually she married Bob Elsworth, our sub-lieutenant. Otherwise the ship was thrown very much on its own resources, which were considerable. I remember Mr Gouffini, our Commissioned Gunner (T) who collected butterflies and moths. He had some wonderful specimens and his cabin was festooned with nets in which were caterpillars under training to be moths. All sorts of games and amusements were thought up for the ship's company.

At one time we landed for field training and pistol competitions. Later when the weather got cold there was skating on a lake in the middle of the island. There were the usual games of football and hockey and the skittle alleys were popular. These had been set up all along the all-red route from England to the Far East. They differed from the modern ten-pin bowls in that the bowls had no hand holds and were of varying sizes from small to enormous. You took your pick. Much-needed beer was available. It was a lot of fun.

One day Hugh Knollys and I went over to the mainland to have a look. The sampan man refused to go so we packed into the ferry, full of Chinese, now in their winter garments. Many of these northerners were big fellows who looked even bigger in their padded clothes. One man had on a superb pair of bearskin trousers which I envied. The walled city was medieval and attractive if you didn't look too closely. There was a military band with a raggle-taggle crew who didn't look as though they would be too much opposition to the tough Japs, who had not yet landed in this area. We felt that they were holding back because of the presence of our large cruiser. We sent up a patrol flying boat every day to keep an eye on their ships hovering offshore. Every now and then a destroyer would enter the bay for no apparent purpose. When at last we abandoned our base in 1941 we heard that any Chinese who had worked for us or were known to be friendly were beheaded on the jetty.

It was now that three of our midshipmen developed malaria. It turned out that they had gone on a picnic in a whaler at Hong Kong and had slept on the beach. Larry Herrick who was in the party had slept in the boat and escaped. In the middle of November, we spent a wakeful night.

Relations with the Japanese navy were worsening as they felt they must show some muscle to the army who were the popular heroes at home and were already about as unpleasant as they could be. There was an intelligence report that there might be an attack without warning on Hong Kong and Singapore. Although this seemed unlikely, we closed up at action stations for the night, ready for what might befall. Nothing did. But Pearl Harbor showed that we had been wise.

TSINGTAO AGAIN

A day or two later we left for Tsingtao as the weather started to turn frigid. The local situation was tense because the Japanese were expected to come at any time. Leave was somewhat restricted but I was able to go out on a ride with about thirty horsemen. We were able to use the ponies left by the Japs when they evacuated the town a while ago. They were splendid little 'griffins' which went flat out over fields and rocks and didn't seem to tire. I was no horseman, but managed to stay on board while the animal followed the crowd. It was an exhilarating afternoon in open country around the old German forts and up

95

to some recent Chinese trenches which appeared to have been abandoned. Altogether it was an odd situation, riding between two combatant nations who were engaged in an undeclared war. But we had to be careful not to get involved or in a situation where the Japanese could complain or be nastier than usual.

Meanwhile the Chinese peasants looked impassively at us foreign devils riding over their country and through their villages which were as primitive as ours had been in the Middle Ages. Fun, when you're nineteen years old. Later we had a splendid gymkhana, all on Japanese horses. There were races of all descriptions, British vs. American, bearded sailors and so on. I entered a steeplechase but couldn't get my horse to go over the jumps and, going around them, came in well but was disqualified. We had again made friends with our opposite numbers in the USS *Marblehead* which had recently arrived to relieve the *Augusta*.

One day on our way to the racecourse we passed the funeral of three Chinese sanitation men who had accidentally let off a grenade while removing it from a Japanese owned building which had been prepared for demolition. I cannot do better than to quote my midshipman's journal:

> *A very elaborate procession headed by a group of children carrying banners; next came a large band of sanitation men in uniform, advancing slowly, step by step. Their band followed playing a hideous but very European dirge. Then there were the official and professional mourners dressed in white robes. They wept and lamented and stopped periodically to kneel in the road. Behind them marched a small guard with a brightly coloured paper shrine in their midst, carried by a few staggering coolies. The bier, covered with red and green streamers, progressed with great pomp along the middle of the road with an escort of cars,*

taxis and onlookers of every description. The victims certainly received more attention as a result of their inefficiency than they ever had in their lifetime.

Meanwhile the undeclared war still went on and I seem to have taken a rather defeatist view of China's prospects, believing that after the loss of Nanking they would do better to capitulate. I was wrong. In the event they never did and the war continued until the Japanese defeat, mainly by the Americans, British and Australians eight years later. In the middle of December there were several serious incidents in which the Japs sank the USS *Panay* and shelled HMS *Ladybird* in the Yangtze. For once an apology was wrung out of the Japanese Admiral, Hasegawa. Nanking fell and although we didn't know it at the time horrible atrocities were committed by the Japanese army. We continued to await developments at Tsingtao amid a rather eerie calm.

On December 18th this calm was shattered by a series of heavy explosions ashore. The Chinese were blowing up the Japanese-owned factories and buildings before evacuating their troops from the city, as part of their scorched-earth policy. We made preparations to evacuate our civilians as well as the local Germans, Russians and other denominations who had no warships present. The burning factories made a spectacular sight by night and it wasn't long before we were allowed to go ashore to have a look around. The inner harbour had been blocked by sinking junks and small steamers and many wretched Chinese were on their way out with all their belongings onto wooden carts. Many hoped to get out by sea. There was quite a lot of looting. Looters who were caught were summarily executed and each day a cart came around and deposited dead bodies which had been shot or decapitated on all the main crossroads in town. Each one had a little white towel attached saying why he had been done to death. Nobody seemed to take much notice and even I got used to it. They were half a world away from our own lives.

On board, things went on according to plan. The two Hughs and I were doing our Engineering course. It was interesting, and had the advantage in this weather of being down in the warm boiler and engine rooms. I do think that in this ship we got an excellent grounding in service life and some good examples to follow. By now there was a curfew at 1900 daily. The inner harbours had been blocked. The foreign communities got ready to be evacuated. There was some agitation in the local English language press, which felt that we should have landed sailors to protect our nationals. They seemed to be unaware that Tsingtao was not a Treaty port, and that we could not treat it as such and land armed men on the soil of a sovereign country. In fact, no harm came to the British until the Japanese attacked Pearl Harbor and Hong Kong. Had we needed to evacuate our people we would probably have had to take the Germans and French as well. The saddest were the White Russians who had fled the revolution and had no one to protect them.

CHRISTMAS

On Christmas Day the curfew was lifted for westerners. We spent the morning on board going around the ingeniously decorated messdecks. Lots were drawn to give each other gifts which had to be extemporised as well. *Suffolk* being a most happy ship, we had a merry time with the sailors and had to avoid little gifts of illegal rum. Then there was lunch in our respective messes, winding up in the afternoon in time to go ashore before dusk. Three of us had dinner with a German family in Tsingtao. I wish I could remember their names. They gave us a superb meal of goose and wine, and one would never have imagined going to war with them. Next day there was a great gymkhana using Japanese horses followed by much feasting and drinking. The day after that there was another holiday when some of us tried to go and see the destroyed Japanese buildings. The driver refused to take us so we explored the old German forts instead. These were still formidable though they had been overcome in 1914. The Chinese made no attempt to use them in the current war. Shortly afterwards the *Dorsetshire* arrived to relieve us and we set off at high speed to get to Hong Kong for the New Year, arriving on December 31st. As far as I can remember I was too tired to go ashore to see the New Year in but hearing the ritual sixteen bells struck and wondering what 1938 would have to offer. *Suffolk* was all ready to sound her siren, but as the flagship remained silent, so must we.

Our stay in Hong Kong was brief, designed only for a rest and a change from keeping an eye on the Nips. So, after only a week we set off north again to Tsingtao. By now it was cold up there and we found that there was a formidable Japanese fleet off the port. They had just landed from the sea, having evidently gone through the motions of assault landings, although there was no opposition. Good practice though. The modern cruiser *Ashigara* was there, flying the flag of Admiral Toyoda. She was quite a familiar sight, having been at the review at Spithead. She was to be sunk at the end of the war by a British submarine [T-class *Trenchant* on 8 June 1945]. Meanwhile they were studiously impolite, keeping our Officer of the Guard waiting on their cold quarterdeck for twenty minutes. I was by now running our motor boat again and lay off waiting in the snow. There were also half a dozen destroyers, sinister looking as ever, a mass of transports painted black and landing craft of many kinds.

ARMY OF OCCUPATION

A couple of days later the Japanese army entered the town. I was fortunate enough to be ashore and saw some of them coming down one of the main streets. It was a sight I shall not forget: those officers on horseback with their distinctive little khaki caps, looking for all the world like an arrogant conquering horde. Genghis Khan came to mind. Many of them wore glasses and nasty little moustaches. Their sturdy-looking soldiers looked cheerful and rotund and tough. I'm glad I never had to meet them face to face in combat. In the event there was little trouble and they soon had iron control of the place. Although they were 'difficult' towards us – arresting our signal party on the pier, and so on – they did not interfere with our civilians and it was soon clear that there was no longer any requirement for *Suffolk* to be standing by to evacuate them. So after quite a short stay we left for Wei Hai Wei.

LAST DAYS IN CHINA

We spent a full month there in mid-winter; quite a change from the summer life. There was snow on the ground, ten degrees of frost and the sea froze in shallow waters. The Japs were still hovering in the offing but hadn't landed yet. There was little for our sailors to do ashore. We played some hockey on a frozen field, skated and walked. On one memorable Saturday six of us went over to the mainland to shoot wildfowl. We walked a long way over the frozen land past medieval villages. We did sight a field full of fat geese which turned out to be shy and wily. The Gunner, Mr Moody, shot our only one. We did bag a hare and some pheasants. At one moment I suddenly realized that the lock-on part of my shotgun was missing. Loss of this would have been a disaster as it was virtually irreplaceable. The gun was a good one, given to me by my mother's great friend Violet Mayo-Robson. It had belonged to her father, Sir Arthur, and had shot much game in Africa in the old days. I carefully backtracked in the snow and was lucky enough to find the missing part about half a mile back. I had to hurry to catch up with the rest of the party and make the boat. A super day.

This was really my swan song in the 'old' China. I had loved every minute of it. Sometimes I wonder what Wei Hai Wei is like nowadays. Is it a naval base? Is it deserted? Have the tourists heard of it yet? I hope not. [Today, Weihai is a thriving port city with a mixed economy of light industries, fishing, tourism and a university. It is also a minor base for the People's Liberation Army Navy.] One of my last memories is of flying the Japanese flag on their National Day, for which they thanked us. They were oddly hostile or friendly and one never knew which it was to be. When our commander went over to call on one of their auxiliary warships, our boat's crew were regaled with apples and pictures of geisha girls. They were just as likely to keep you waiting in the snow for twenty minutes. Our departure for Hong Kong was accompanied by a final fusillade of firecrackers by our sampan men. I wonder how many of them survived the coming occupation.

LAST DAYS

The passage south had a bit of everything. Cold and calm to start with, then quite rough, then warmer, and finally we had to feel our way into Hong Kong in fog. Next day, Captain Phillips, who had been popular and successful, was relieved by Captain C.S. Sandford. For some regrettable reason we christened him 'Poopdeck Pappy'. I wasn't in the ship long enough to form any other opinion of him. A week after our arrival in Hong Kong our final exams as midshipmen took place: ship construction, signals and the major one, seamanship. We appeared before a board consisting of a captain and three commanders (rather like a court martial) on board the *Adventure*. The exam, as far as I can remember, was oral and not too demanding; we had well prepared. All three of us passed and I got a First Class which I had hoped and tried for. Otherwise our last days were occupied going to sea for day and night shoots which were only fairly good. But, having heard that we had passed, all that remained was to leave the ship and await passage to England in the Blue Funnel liner *Hector*. I had had a wild idea of trying to get home by rail via Siberia (our mails used to come this way). But finance reared its head and so it was the old all-red route home. As for my further doings, Behold, are they not written in my Memoirs of 'How I won the War' [published as *In Action with Destroyers*] and later, 'How I lost the Peace'?

PART II

The Life of Rear-Admiral John Lee-Barber

by Anthony J. Cumming

CHAPTER 1

JOHN LEE-BARBER

Part of John Lee-Barber's early naval service was on China's Yangtze river a few months after the Japanese attack on Manchuria, a tragedy that first exposed the impotence of the League of Nations and encouraged the expansionist ambitions of Germany and Italy. Since 1927 there was also a civil war raging between the communists and government forces, with both the USSR and USA providing support for the government. Chungking was the first Chinese inland port opened to foreigners. Later it became Generalissimo Chiang Kai-shek's provisional capital. Sadly, the only record of Johnny's China service written by him exists in a single letter to his family.

Johnny was born on 16 April 1905, at Lowestoft. As a boy, 'he was drawn to the sight of First World War destroyers going about their wartime missions in the North Sea. It determined a career in the Royal Navy and for the boisterous and informal lifestyle that service in these ships offered,' stated Captain Michael Hennessy at Johnny's funeral in 1996.[10]

From the age of 13, Johnny began training at the Royal Naval College, Osborne, on the Isle of Wight, before it closed in 1921. This must have been a sad occasion for the cadets, Osbourne having been the magnificent royal palace so beloved of Queen Victoria and Prince Albert, with its sweeping view of the Solent. Along with most of the other boys, he then transferred to the Royal Naval College, Dartmouth, today the Britannia Royal

Naval College. Most of his training and early service after that was in destroyers — as a midshipman on the V-class *Vidette*, sub-lieutenant on the W-class *Wessex* and lieutenant on the W-class *Wakeful* and V-class *Vimiera*. Johnny could hardly have imagined that the V, W and I classes were destined to be the destroyers holding the line in the dark days of 1940 some twenty years later. One notable exception during his training was the Insect class *Falcon*, a flat-bottomed gunboat built by Yarrow Shipbuilders in 1931. *Falcon* served on the Yangtze River for many years and was finally gifted to the Chinese Navy in 1942. Johnny served on *Falcon* during 1932/3 during a period of rising tensions, with the Japanese army controlling a large part of the middle and lower river and the communist Chinese National Revolutionary Army holding much of the north bank of the middle river.[11]

A letter to his family in July 1932 written at Chungking (now Chongqing) painted a vivid picture of life on the Yangtze at this time. 'Chungking is a very large and completely unhygienic city situated on the left on north bank of the River Yangtze a distance of 1,400 miles from Woosung.' To his evident relief, *Falcon* lay on the opposite bank where English and other foreign firms occupied most of the foreshore and the expatriates lived in 'very fine houses'. He continued, 'There is quite a good little club with two tennis courts, a billiard room and an up to date library, a fair-sized bar with enough dice boxes for all the members to play simultaneously.' There was also time to explore the countryside on the local ponies. 'Riding them is the most hair-raising thing I have ever done. When you get up into the hills back of the foreshore you find yourself galloping along a path of no more than three feet wide which is winding all the time with a drop of anything up to 80 feet on one side of you. Believe me, China breeds brave men.'

These problems aside, it was very desirable for the foreign community to move up into their summer bungalows as Johnny reported 'a shade temperature of between 99 and 101, knocking 'the stuffing out of you a bit'. Another day, he had to attend a Chinese lunch party, 'the most awful affair that it has ever been my lot to attend. We had Chinese food which is perfectly bloody, sharks fin soup, grilled chicken's feet, duck skin varnished and dipped in some peculiarly revolting sauce being amongst an orgy of unpleasant dishes, after it we went for a motor drive on the only road in the province and I thought I would throw up at any moment.' Of the military situation, Johnny wrote, 'The latest excitements on the river are the success of the Communists on the banks of the Middle river i.e. Ichang to Yochow, where they have defeated the nationalist troops all along the line, the disappearance of the Captain of an American merchant ship, and another total loss of a steamer on the Upper River. However up here in Chungking all is peace and quiet, we expect to be here till early September then go down to Shanghai to refit.'[12]

He returned to destroyers and in 1937 took command of the W-class destroyer *Witch*. In May 1937, Ordinary Seaman (later Lt. Commander) Harry Wardle joined *Witch* recalling she had a scratch crew with only four officers. Johnny soon realised Harry was 'someone with a great future ahead of him' and in 1994 wrote the foreword to Harry's book about life in the Royal Navy. *Witch* was then part of the Irish Patrol based at Queenstown (Cobh) in the Irish Free State and Queenstown was one of three Irish deep-water treaty ports playing a major part in the first Battle of the Atlantic during the 1914-18 War. However, by 1938 the Royal Navy's use of the three treaty ports had become such a thorny issue in Anglo-Irish relations, the British government handed them over to the Irish Free State – a concession that did not please most naval personnel. In the event, the loss made little difference to the later Battle of the Atlantic, as international trade was conducted through the North West Approaches. Queenstown, though a far more salubrious city than Chungking, was nevertheless poor by European standards.

According to Harry, 'Poverty was rife, which meant we, with our 14 shillings a week, were rich, and to our delight very much in demand by the local girls, leading to trouble with the boys.' This in turn could only have resulted in problems for Johnny and the other officers. One of Harry's problems was keeping the quarterdeck clean after Johnny's dog. 'He [Jamie] would sniff around Y gun and then walk onto my clean corticene deck, which we tried to keep polished, with oily paws.'[13] Despite this, Jamie was popular and 'much loved by all on board but he was definitely the Captain's dog'. Jamie's service as mascot began in 1933, and at the time of his passing Jamie had served on six destroyers. 'He was deeply and sincerely mourned by his human messmates, and his name is on the Mascot Club Roll of Honour.[14] In fact, Johnny had two dogs named Jamie – both white bull-terriers and ships' mascots, but were probably less well-liked ashore than afloat. When Johnny came home on leave with his second dog, Jamie, 'attacked the postman or any man who came with deliveries' and Johnny's young daughters remained wary of him.[15]

Harry left *Witch* in September 1937 but met Johnny and Jamie again in 1939 when Johnny was captain of *Griffin* and Wardle was a Leading Torpedo Operator (L.T.O.). Later, Johnny took command of the A-class *Ardent* destined to sink in a heroic attack on the German heavy ships *Scharnhorst* and *Gneisenau* in June 1940. By then, *Ardent* was commanded by Lt. Cdr. J.F. Barker, D.S.C., R.N.

In 1938, Johnny took command of *Griffin* where he and Jamie were to spend their next three years. His new ship was built by Vickers-Armstrong in Barrow-in-Furness in the mid-1930s. She boasted four 4.7-inch Mark IX guns and two quadruple 0.5 Vickers Mark III machine guns for air defence. There were also two quadruple torpedo mounts, a depth charge rail, and two throwers.[16] The main weakness was in the field of anti-aircraft armament, meaning that in the coming war, *Griffin* would rely heavily on Johnny's ability to manoeuvre the ship away from enemy bombs.

A study of his reporting officer's confidential reports over several decades reveal a capable, loyal, and popular officer running happy, efficient ships. Frequently acknowledged were his considerable leadership skills and ability to handle a ship, with his popularity resting upon the respect of both subordinates and superior officers. He got things done because he inspired those who served beneath him and only drove them when it was necessary. John Lee Barber eventually rose to flag rank; his daughter Victoria maintained that the main reason he never became a member of the Naval Staff was his disdain for paperwork, preferring to spend his professional time at sea. Not that Johnny's spells as Correspondence Officer aboard V-class destroyer HMS *Vimiera* or any other judgment on his 'administrative ability' confirmed a specific weakness in this area, though his superior's reports did occasionally hint at it. He was a seaman at heart.

The only negative comment worthy of mention was what some superiors considered an over-sensitivity to criticism. But the only officer to make anything of this was the eccentric Lt. Commander Roland F.B. Swinley who wrote of Lt. Lee-Barber in 1929: 'An undisciplined young officer who has never been properly broken in'. He thought Johnny 'undisciplined, temperamental, moody and inconsistent' and 'far too familiar at all times with his subordinate officers and men'. Swinley was an old school autocrat who disapproved of any familiarity between the ranks and, as Alec's wartime memoirs suggest, seems to have had an obnoxious tyrannical streak. In fairness, he rated Johnny's professional ability, judgment, and initiative highly, but with his attitude for paperwork in mind, perhaps there was some small truth in the remark 'He could be an exceptional officer if he would not confine himself to trying only at the things which particularly interest him.'[17] Nevertheless, once the war started, Johnny quickly gained a reputation as 'a very excellent destroyer captain' and a 'most successful sub-divisional leader' who was also 'cool and determined in the face of the enemy'.[18]

Official reports aside, Johnny's reputation with colleagues grew steadily, with G.G. Connell describing him as a 'splendid character ... a man regarded with considerable affection by his contemporaries; he possessed an attractive relaxed personality and a natural ability as a leader of men.' Johnny was unconventional, 'easy-going and unflappable to the point of appearing to be rather lazy ... and his presence at any gathering was much sought after'. His devoted companion, Jamie, the [second] white bull terrier, was said by this source to be 'quite unmoved by gunfire, bomb near-misses or underwater explosions; the dog accompanied his master to the sea cabin and remained there on the bridge close to J.L.B. for the entire time the ship was at sea.'[19]

In 1939, Johnny married Sue le Gallais of St. Hellier, Jersey, at Alexandria, with whom he would have two daughters. Their honeymoon lasted only a weekend until he was again sent to sea. They remained happily married up until Sue's death in 1976.

CHAPTER 2

THE WAR

Alec returned from the Far East aboard the Blue Funnel liner *Hector* and in 1938 continued his training at Portsmouth where he achieved six examination 'firsts' including torpedoes, gunnery navigation and signals – excellent for his promotion prospects. Later training was interrupted by the Munich Crisis of 1938 and Alec found himself posted to the old destroyer *Sturdy* where he remained until the crisis had passed. His shortened courses ended before Christmas 1938, and in January 1939 he disembarked from the troopship *Nevasa* to serve with the First Destroyer Flotilla aboard the G-class destroyer *Griffin* at Malta as a sub-lieutenant.

Here he met his new captain, Lt. Commander John Lee-Barber, for the first time. Johnny lent Alec some civilian clothes to go ashore in. 'A small matter perhaps, but not many Captains would have done it,' he wrote later.[20] Shortly afterwards, Alec was Officer of the Day and so missed Malta's carnival day, 18th February 1939. The fireworks, street bunting, and religious parades were always spectacular, but before the war these celebrations were notorious for drunken behaviour among servicemen. 'As cabaret dancer Christina Ratcliffe noted, before the war Malta was a "boozer's paradise". Spirits were sixpence a tot and beer fourpence a bottle.'[21] To miss such an event was particularly hard on a young man wanting to celebrate his 21st birthday, but he made the best of it with a bottle of champagne and some classical music on the ship's radiogram – the integrated home audio system of the day. Later that evening, a seaman roused Alec from his armchair to tell him the captain was returning. As it was his duty to greet him, Alec went up on deck but could only see a *dghaisa* (a gondola type rowing boat) without a passenger. Puzzled, he looked around and after a moment saw someone swimming towards the ladder. It was of course, his slightly inebriated captain having fallen from the boat as the boatman pushed off from the quay. With commendable *sang-froid*, Johnny climbed the ladder and greeted Alec as if nothing out of the ordinary had happened and with his mess-undress dripping disappeared below for a hot bath.[22]

Destroyer captains were of a certain breed, with similarities to their RAF Fighter Command contemporaries, and the crews shared a special camaraderie owing to the relatively small size of ship and crew. It was claimed by Admiral Sir Herbert Richmond – a leading naval historian of the 1930s – that the introduction of destroyers 'from the very start encouraged the young officers who commanded these craft to take risks and not shirk responsibility, and wisely [the Admiralty] turned a blind eye to the mishaps that were on occasion the result of zeal and not of carelessness'.[23]

Torpedo-boat destroyers first emerged in the late nineteenth century as an antidote to the small, fast torpedo boats of the 1880s that naval strategists expected might well annihilate the battle fleet in a future war. These evolved from an 1892 specification requested by the dynamic Third Sea Lord Rear-Admiral Jackie Fisher for a gun-carrying vessel capable of making a continuous 27 knots. Consequently, six so-called '27-knotters' emerged from shipyards displacing a mere 260/280 tons and carrying one 12-pounder and three 6-pounder guns plus three torpedo tubes. These 'A' class boats were the first proper destroyers.[24]

Organised into flotillas the destroyers took part in fleet exercises, and in the First World War they found new roles, most importantly as hunters of U-boats. So useful did they become, the destroyer was the most common class of warship in the Royal Navy at this time. There were rarely enough of these warships around in the Second World War and in the early phase of the conflict the shortage was particularly acute. Destroyers undertook convoy escort, anti-submarine work and provided protective screens for larger ships against submarines, torpedo boats and to a lesser extent air attack. As for the first half of the conflict, very few destroyers had effective armament against German dive-bombers, the Junkers Ju.87 and Ju.88. The infamous Ju.87 Stuka was capable of diving at steep angles and outside the arc of most destroyer gun-mountings.

Johnny and Alec's wartime adventures on *Griffin* are detailed in *In Action with Destroyers*; to avoid duplication only an outline of their service will be given here. *Griffin* served in home waters during the so-called Phoney War of 1939-40, a period of intense strain and discomfort for both the Royal Navy and Merchant Navy owing to the devastating impact of German magnetic mines upon shipping. These losses included *Griffin's* sister ships *Gipsy* and *Grenville*. With that threat largely countered by degaussing techniques *Griffin* later took part in the Norway Campaign of 1940 where Admiral Sir Charles Forbes' Home Fleet attempted to thwart the German invasion of that country. Owing largely to intelligence failures on the part of the British and the German *B-Dienst* service holding the initiative by deducing Allied warship dispositions by reading the strength and direction of their signal traffic and reading several British naval codes, the *Kriegsmarine* successfully landed troops along various points on the Norwegian coast. Despite a resounding British naval victory at Narvik and the campaign decimating the German surface fleet – dooming any German attempt to invade Great Britain in 1940 – Norway was a German victory won by the effective projection of German airpower against Allied land forces and superior naval intelligence. Johnny's efforts during this campaign of difficult embarkations and re-embarkations earned him the Polish Cross of Valour.

One incident during this campaign needs covering in much greater detail than Alec has previously given concerning the capture of the German armed trawler *Polares*. Thanks to the actions of *Griffin*'s captain and crew, the Government Code and Cypher School at Bletchley Park obtained their first opportunity to break into the German Enigma naval code. Although Alec's war memoirs alluded to the controversies surrounding the capture of the German armed trawler *Polares,* the following account written from a variety of official and other sources provides a more detailed justification for their actions.

CHAPTER 3

POLARES

On 26 April, and shortly after *Griffin* left Aandalsnes where she had assisted in the evacuation of British troops, a signal from the A-class destroyer *Arrow* alerted British ships to the danger posed by armed German trawlers disguised as neutrals.[25] Thus began the *Polares* incident – an episode which on the one hand led to an important breakthrough in an intelligence war the Allies were still losing but on the other threatened to sink both Alec and Johnny's careers. At the time *Polares* fell into British hands, nobody aboard *Griffin* knew anything about ENIGMA machines or the ULTRA messages that came from them and any judgement of this affair must consider this fact carefully.

It began with a fight between British ships and the German armed trawler *Shelwig (Schiff 37)* in the course of which the cruiser *Birmingham* sank *Schiff 37* but not before the German ship rammed the *Arrow* causing her serious damage.[26] Just as this information arrived, Johnny found a trawler steaming northwards and flying the Dutch flag. Roused from his bunk, Alec received Johnny's orders to board a suspected enemy ship. Wary of torpedoes, Johnny manoeuvred *Griffin* out of the trawler's likely line of torpedo fire. Alec jumped into a whaler with Johnny Blackmore, Ian Kenyon and half a dozen sailors. As they approached in a rough sea – 'wind force 5 to 6 and Sea 43' – it became apparent that the trawler was not what she first appeared, displaying an obvious canvas mock-up abaft (to the rear of) her funnel and more men on deck than any trawler seemed to need. Soon the boarding party was alongside with the whaler heaving up and down. The first sailor encountered – probably Georges Schwenke – 'announced: "German ship"'. Now they saw that the canvas mock-up concealed a gun and fishing nets covering two torpedo tubes. *Griffin* had intercepted

Polares (Schiff 26) on a mission to land stores and ammunition to Narvik and lay magnetic mines in Narvik Fjord.[27]

Summoned on deck at gunpoint by the boarders, a fierce argument broke out between what appeared to be the supervising naval party, some German army passengers, and the original fishing crew. It later transpired that the crew were mainly reservists of low morale, and despite Oberleutnant zur Zee Heinz Engelein's Iron Cross, they held scant respect for their captain.[28] Johnny Blackmore went below to the engine room and Ian Kenyon went forward to round up the crew and prevent any scuttling attempt. In the process, Kenyon stumbled and accidentally fired his revolver on the bridge quietening the fractious Germans who did not realise where the shot had come from. However, they had already thrown overboard the Enigma machine, charts, and codebooks. A canvas bag floated on the surface as the prize crew had pulled towards *Polares*, but because of the turbulent sea they were unable to grapple it. The prompt action of Gunner (T) Florrie Foord diving on the end of a line from *Griffin*'s quarterdeck recovered some valuable material – a bag containing one codebook and some ciphering forms. This was not without mishap. On hauling in, Florrie went under but came to the surface still clutching the bag. The crew threw another line that he grabbed with one hand, and after losing his grip in the freezing water, Florrie submerged again, still holding the bag. Fortunately, he managed to get a line made into a lasso over his shoulders and found himself hauled aboard. Johnny wrote, 'But for the prompt and tenacious action of Mr Foord, it would undoubtedly not have been saved.'[29] For the recovery, he subsequently received a well-deserved – if inadequate – M.B.E.

Alec told the German crew that if they were to scuttle the ship there would be no attempt to rescue them.[30] Probably because of this threat, Schwenke warned him that the after-hatch leading to the magazine was booby-trapped. Alec took the warning seriously – a time fuze was later found but it had to be lit to go off – and exchanged those Germans who weren't required to man the ship for British sailors.[31] At this point,

Johnny was obliged to aid the Aandalsnes anti-aircraft guard ship, the Black Swan-class sloop *Flamingo* – then under heavy attack – leaving Alec, his men and the remaining German crew to take the prize back to Scapa Flow.

Now in command of his first ship, Alec discovered all the charts and navigational equipment missing, apart from an old herring fishing chart. However, this was sufficient to plot a rough course for the Shetlands south-westwards without the aid of proper navigational instruments but using a setsquare as parallel ruler.[32] The British sailors were outnumbered and vigilant but Alec remembered the trip home as an enjoyable experience with 'a big fat Bavarian chef' cooking up large meals of bacon and eggs'. The trip took two days during which Alec attempted to tidy up the mess left behind by the Germans. They sighted Muckle Flugga in the Shetlands and changed course to avoid outlying rocks and found themselves well south of Wick after 'Sparks' brought the radio to life and a D/F (direction finding) bearing was taken. Cliffs appeared out of the gloom and the ship ran into a heavy cross-swell off land causing the coal to shift in the bunkers and an alarming starboard list. This required some hard shovelling on the part of the German stokers.[33]

Eventually *Polares* entered Scapa Flow, passing his old ship, the flagship *Rodney*, at Sunday divisions and making for Gutter Sound, finally tying up alongside *Griffin*. Sixty years after these events, and long after writing his memoirs, Alec became aware of publicity in books and articles deriving from official reports that 'rather told against me'. In a statement reproduced in Appendix I, he wrote firstly '...was the fact that I entered Scapa Flow past the assembled fleet flying the White Ensign above the German naval flag.' As far as Alec was concerned, 'at the time it seemed to me to be a time-honoured naval custom from the French, American and German wars. It never occurred to me that a humble fishing trawler carrying ammunition and stores could be such a valuable intelligence prize.'[34] However, from the perspective of Rear-Admiral John Godfrey the Director of Naval Intelligence (D.N.I.D.), this small conceit was a security lapse potentially revealing that *Polares*, rather than sunk outright, was now in British hands along with all her intelligence material. By chance, a Universal film crew filmed the 'triumphant' entry but the film was confiscated and not shown. Such a realisation would have caused the *Kriegsmarine* to change their codes. However, in the event there was no breach of security as the Germans remained unaware of what had occurred.[35] Unfortunately, nobody at Scapa Flow thought it necessary to receive *Polares* before entering harbour and then place it in a secure and discreet berth.[36]

The second charge – of looting the ship – was more serious and rankled with Alec and Johnny for the rest of their lives. Here, Alec questioned the veracity of an official report submitted by a 'retired Commander', identified in official records as Commander F.S. Piper, O.B.E. – see Appendix III. 'Almost his first act was to ask me to find a screwdriver and proceeded to help himself to a barometer which was fixed to the bulkhead. Thus, his later "evidence" to the Port Admiral is, to me, highly suspect, although [Rear] Admiral [Sir Hugh] Binney seems to have trusted him implicitly.' Alec recalled, 'He had problems bringing the vessel to an anchor, during which manoeuvre he had some of our men to assist until a scratch crew of minesweeping men took over.' It seems likely to me that these people must have done the breaking in which was reported, though the statement of the Sub-Lieutenant [later Lt. Commander Wilfred Louis Gerard Dutton, R.N.R.] who took over later denies anything like this.' The reported chaos was the result of the German crew's surprise who 'grabbed what they could when we boarded and [as described above] the ship had rolled heavily, throwing loose gear all over the place.'[37]

Piper's report of 20 May 1940 to the port admiral, Binney, painted a chaotic picture: 'I went below, and found the mess-decks littered with gear, lockers smashed open, doors wrenched off, and members of the crew of HMS Griffin taking away every conceivable thing they could carry, and passing them inboard to the Griffin.' Moving on 'down to the engine room and thence to the Wheelhouse ... I ordered men away who were helping themselves to gear, etc.' A little later he boarded *Griffin* 'and, on turning round, found swarms of men from the *Griffin* still helping themselves to things from the Polares'. Equally damaging was Piper's accusation that at approximately 20.00 on 28 April he found Engelein's private apartments locked and 'on looking through the grating the contents looked in order in the sleeping cabin and office' and at 21.00 he took charge of the ship and took it to Myres Bay. The following day at approximately 13.00 and in company with Dutton, they found these compartments 'broken into and pillaged'. Piper opined this took place when *Polares* was alongside the *Griffin* and the hatchway broken down to get to the medical stores' cupboard next to the captain's cabin. He caught a Sick Berth Attendant with medical stores just before casting off and ordered their return, drawing an apology from *Griffin*'s Medical Officer.[38] However, there is an apparent conflict of evidence on the state of these apartments, as Binney's report to Admiral Forbes states in paragraph 3 that he was aboard *Polares* with Rear Admiral Lyster on the afternoon of 29 April and they looked into the Captain's cabin: 'I should not describe its state as having been looted.'[39]

Alec admitted to letting the crew help themselves to the rest of the rations and 'a souvenir German sailor's cap, having made sure that nothing of importance was taken'. Johnny did likewise, but restricted this to the mess deck and under the first lieutenant's supervision. Later, Johnny was to receive a letter expressing their Lordship's displeasure over the incident – a serious black mark. Alec was grateful Johnny's report exonerated him from blame by submitting an opinion that *Polares* must have been 'considerably rummaged' after she left *Griffin*. There are indications in paragraphs 5 and 10 of a report from Lt. Pennell, the NID representative supporting this – see Appendix II. It suggests Dutton's crew and others looted the ship. Dutton's men were 'taken from minesweeping drifters' and were not regular naval personnel. Pennell mentioned that 'a number of ships had gone alongside for various reasons, and it is probable that they removed small objects as trophies.'[40] Piper's report, dated over a fortnight later, needed to address this as it questioned both his and Dutton's supervision of the ship. It is interesting that Piper undermined Pennell's account by pointedly contradicting his claim to have assisted Lt. Glenny to render a mine safe by stating unequivocally that his Group Officer, 'volunteered and <u>alone</u> assisted Lieutenant Glenny to render all the mines safe'. Pennell spoke directly to Admiral Binney, Flag Officer Orkneys, and Shetlands, shortly after his arrival but it is unknown whether he made any accusations against members of his staff at this time. Binney's report of 24 May suggested that Pennell was 'over-wrought' and 'this condition coloured his report' implying an exchange of strong words over responsibility for the looting. He denied that any 'ships other than the [T-class submarine] "TRITONIA" went alongside and only such boats as were essential.' Binney also stated, 'I am convinced that no looting was carried out by the officers and men under his [Piper's] command.'[41]

However, Johnny accepted that 'in allowing my ship's company to board and take away souvenirs from the prize I committed an error of judgment and contravened the Naval Discipline Act. This error I deeply regret.'[42] He did not want the boarding party blamed for the *Polares'* condition, and to this Forbes agreed, though given the weight of evidence before him, he was not prepared to let Johnny off scot-free. For his part, Alec maintained that all the missing material went overboard before he set foot on deck, and there is no reason to doubt him on this point. For all this, some sense of fair play prevailed at the Admiralty because Alec finally received a Mention in Despatches for his part in the capture and neither Alec nor Johnny's careers seem to have suffered. Readers should examine the reports at Appendices I-VII and decide whether or not the officers at Scapa Flow closed ranks; and it must be borne in mind that no Board of Enquiry tested these statements.

Very few German warships fell into Allied hands during this early phase of the war and the Allies desperately needed to capture the German naval codebooks and an Enigma machine with its rotors set for action. Unfortunately, proper post-capture procedures for these situations had yet to be developed. On 15

April 1940, only eleven days before, British ships forced submarine U49 to the surface but without recovering any code material. As a result, Admiral Forbes circulated the first instructions on the importance of seizing such material and how to go about this.[43] It is, however, unclear exactly when he circulated them and whether it was possible to have them immediately implemented given the situation prevailing at the time. Some post-war history books have been overly critical in this matter.[44]

On the positive side, the cipher material recovered by Florrie together with the papers picked up by N.I.D. from the deck detritus went to the government code-breakers of Bletchley Park who went on to break the Enigma cipher for 22-27 April 1940, but only for these five days. It enabled the British to read their first German Naval Enigma message on 17 May 1940 and one of the documents laid out the sending procedures for scrambling the messages. Armed with this knowledge, the cryptologist Alan Turing was eventually able to devise 'an ingenious, though long-winded method of breaking the naval Enigma code' known as Banburismus.[45] The next six months yielded few results, and it would take much more work and the capture of further material before the initiative passed firmly into British hands during August 1941.[46] Even so, it is reasonable to state that the actions of *Griffin*'s captain and crew in capturing the *Polares* alongside the work of Alan Turing and others made the cracking of the Enigma code possible.[47]

On a more trivial note, Alec was clearly irritated at having to hand in the binoculars given to him by Heinz Engelein. Johnny was sympathetic but there was nothing he could do as the order came from Admiral Forbes. Others were more fortunate. When U110 was captured by Commander Joe Baker-Cresswell (formerly Alec's snotty's nurse aboard *Rodney*) in command of the destroyer *Bulldog* during the Battle of Convoy OB138 in May 1941, his boarding officer was told to bring back some German binoculars. He brought back two swastika-stamped Zeiss pairs, one of which remained in that officer's possession for fifty years. A cap belonging to ace U-boat commander Fritz

Julius Lempe was also recovered and presented to the Imperial war Museum in 2003. This exploit did involve the capture of an Enigma machine.[48]

CHAPTER 4

JOHNNY AND *OPPORTUNE*

Lt. Commander John Lee-Barber was now among those sailors officially recognised for good services since the outbreak of war. Gazetted for the Distinguished Service Order on 11 July 1940, 'For good services in the Royal Navy since the outbreak of War' and 'For his efforts in anti-invasion patrols along the English Channel'.[49] There, and in no small part to Johnny's skilful handling of the ship, *Griffin* survived a particularly determined assault from thirty-six Dornier Do.17 twin-engine bombers, one of many air attacks endured by the crew over the next two and a half years. A few days after his D.S.O., Johnny also received a Mention in Despatches 'for good service in the withdrawal of troops from the Namsos area'.[50]

On 10 May 1940, Johnny received orders to take the ship to Dover with all despatch. The same day, the German Army smashed through the Allied line into Holland, Belgium and France, indirectly bringing about the end of the Norway campaign. Also, on the 10th of May Winston Churchill replaced Neville Chamberlain as prime minister, ironically the result of the failed Norway campaign for which Churchill, as First Lord, was politically responsible. So began the most famous period of the great warlord's life. One of his first acts after the Dunkirk evacuation was to send troops to Brittany, but such was the momentum of the enemy advance that another evacuation was quickly organised. *Griffin* took part in the remarkable rescue of troops and equipment from Brittany known as Operation Aerial and, as mentioned above, served in the English Channel as one of the destroyers protecting merchant shipping from E-boats and the Luftwaffe during the opening phase of the Battle of Britain known as the *Kanalkampf.* So intense was the German pressure on *Griffin*'s base at Dover that the area became known as 'Hellfire Corner'

120

and the naval base was finally forced to close – though it was the only one to do so at this time. *Griffin*'s later Mediterranean service took in actions such as the Battle of Bardia, Battle of Cape Matapan, the Greece Evacuations, and the Battle of Crete, along with supply runs to Tobruk and the Malta convoys. In 1941, Johnny added a bar to his D.S.O. for his actions off Matapan and in Greek waters. In later life, Johnny told his daughter their survival had been down to luck. When pressed further, he told her, 'Well, we discovered if we sent up all our fire-power, the Germans had to drop their bombs from a bit higher. Then we just had time to see them falling and avoid them. At Crete, the Luftwaffe dropped eighteen bombs on them in one hour.'[51]

Although delighted that Johnny received promotion to Commander, Alec was saddened by his captain's departure from *Griffin* in late 1941 to take up a new post as naval advisor to Southern Command Army Headquarters Home Forces. Here, Johnny's army commander reported 'how much he admired the way he threw himself heart and soul into any job he was given'.[52] Following this shore appointment the Admiralty intended he should command the Tribal-class destroyer *Eskimo* but a last minute personnel reshuffle confronted Johnny with a 'pierhead jump' as captain of the new O-class destroyer *Opportune* recently built by John I. Thornycroft, Woolston.[53] By comparison with *Griffin,* and the pre-war destroyers, *Opportune* was well equipped to deal with air attack, possessing four 4-inch guns in high angle gun mountings and four of the reasonably effective 'Chicago Piano' QF-2 pounders.[54]

Johnny was a keen exponent of using Royal Navy Reserve and Royal Naval Volunteer Reserve officers to fill his wardroom and, with only two exceptions, *Opportune* worked up with reserve officers. *Opportune* would eventually become one of eight O-class destroyers, but at the beginning of September 1942 there were only five on active service, with *Oribi* refitting at Immingham making a sixth. All the O-class destroyers ordered in 1939 as part of the War Emergency Programme went to the

Home Fleet's 17th Destroyer Flotilla on 14 August 1942. Johnny was to command from 26 September 1942 until 14 August 1944. Initially, *Opportune* underwent conversion to minelaying before a brief deployment to the East Coast Barrier in October.

The 17th Destroyer Flotilla's first major task was to escort convoys to Russia. Convoys sailed from British ports to support the Soviet war effort since the German invasion of the Soviet Union in 1941. These played a key role when the Soviet Union's survival was uncertain and the Arctic convoys endured throughout the conflict as a tangible symbol of inter-Allied cooperation. Churchill famously called this 'the worst journey in the world' and the convoys became 'a marathon of human and mechanical endurance'.[55] The route took convoys over the top of German-occupied Norway into the Arctic but poor light meant intense navigational and signalling difficulties and the danger of loose floating ice damaging the hulls. It also meant men with steam hoses and hand tools working in sub-zero conditions to remove engulfing ice sheets that if not removed would capsize the ship. All this took a heavy toll on men and machinery with casualties from frostbite and all the miseries of living and working in permanently cold, wet conditions.[56]

The first convoys were unopposed by the Germans, but once they realised the importance of the lifeline, the situation changed. Casualties from German aircraft and submarines increased dramatically – notably when the Germans smashed convoy PQ17 in July 1942 – following the Admiralty's tragically mistaken decision to order the convoy to scatter in the erroneous belief that the battleship *Tirpitz* was closing in. It had been the first substantial joint Anglo-American operation of the war and as such became a keenly felt failure.[57] None of this helped ease the frosty and humourless reception that British crews received from dour Soviet hosts. Soviet hostility had its roots in historical resentment over British support for the White Russians in 1918-19, their perception of British incompetence and dishonesty over the PQ17 disaster, and bitterness over the low quality of some of the equipment sent in the first convoy.

122

Under Johnny's predecessor, Commander Manley Laurence Power, D.S.O., O.B.E., the *Opportune* joined the next convoy sailing in September 1942 as part of the screen for escort carrier *Avenger* and light cruiser *Scylla*.[58] PQ18's passage faced bitter opposition, but the new escort carriers allowed the merchant ships much more air and anti-submarine protection enabling the convoy to make it through to Arkangel. [59]

The grim conditions made it essential for naval morale to seek some diversion at sea, and as it was the captain's responsibility to maintain morale, Johnny purchased a large illustrated Botany encyclopaedia and fostered a wardroom interest in Arctic flowers. The sight of *Opportune*'s officers and ratings carrying flowers and plants when ashore became the target of much rude comment and the identification of collected specimens became an unusual feature of Johnny's alcoholic wardroom social gatherings. Together they identified some 240 species during Johnny's tenure.[60]

As a break from Arctic convoying, and under conditions of the greatest secrecy, *Opportune* sailed from Devonport to Gibraltar as escort for the cruiser *Scylla*. Aboard *Scylla* was Admiral Cunningham, recently appointed as Allied Naval Commander for Operation Torch, the planned invasion of French Morocco and French Algeria. Johnny and *Scylla*'s captain were the only two officers to know their destination. After safely depositing Cunningham at Gibraltar on 1st November both ships took part in anti-invasion exercises with other warships earmarked for the operation, but on the 18th *Opportune* began her voyage back to the U.K. *En route* Johnny was ordered to leave the screen and search for a U-boat reportedly damaged by a Fleet Air Arm Swordfish. U517 had already been scuttled by the time *Opportune* arrived at the reported spot south-west of Ireland but she was in time to rescue fifty-one German submariners.[61] Many years later, on the 50th anniversary of the sinking, U517's former captain, Paul Hartwig, wrote to Johnny to thank him for rescuing the crew and recognising that *Opportune* put herself 'at risk of being sunk by another submarine'. At the time of the rescue, Johnny offered

Hartwig a glass of port in the wardroom. He declined, instead proposing they drink together after the war, 'either in London or in Berlin' depending on the final outcome.[62] By late November 1942, the war was about to swing in favour of the Allies, but it would not have been obvious to those taking part.

Christmas 1942 was a grim affair for the crews anchored at Kola inlet, and for once the traditional frozen Russian hospitality thawed to the extent that Russian Commander-in-Chief Admiral Arseni Golovoko sent his naval choir to regale the confined British crews with traditional Russian carols. This did not suit Johnny at all, so taking charge of a party of drunken officers from *Opportune* and *Matchless*, he had a whaler lowered and equipped it with candle lanterns before setting off on a carol singing expedition to entertain the scattered groups of naval personnel marooned in Murmansk. It was not an unqualified success. Having disturbed a puzzled and threatening Russian sentry at one signal establishment, a sailor shouted down from a window, 'Why don't you lot push off, we work watch and watch and our mates are trying to get some sleep.' Undiscouraged, Johnny's group staggered off to a more appreciative audience of medics, who gratefully partook of their visitors' alcoholic refreshments.[63]

Despite the success of British destroyers in the Battle of the Barents Sea frustrating the attack of German heavy cruisers *Hipper* and *Lützow* on convoy JW51B in December 1942 (and thus forcing a change in German naval strategy away from surface raiders towards U-boats) the British suspended the convoys after March 1943 because shipping resources were urgently required elsewhere. So long as heavy German air and naval forces remained in Norway during the period of continuous summer daylight, the risks were high anyway.[64] The last convoys before summer 1943 were JW53 and RA53; *Opportune* participated in the return convoy, RA53. As it assembled, waves of German bombers homed in on the merchant ships, but on this occasion the defences successfully drove the attackers off. The first four days of sailing passed without incident, but U255 picked up the convoy on the second day remaining in contact with it until an opportunity presented itself. On 5 March, it finally came and U255 charged into the ships sinking one freighter and damaging another. A Ju.88 bombing attack followed, but barrages of anti-aircraft fire – much of it from the destroyers – drove it away. That night the convoy took a battering from storms and the ships began straggling thus enabling U586 to sink a freighter on the 9th. On the 10th U255 finally sank the ship she damaged earlier. The violent weather claimed both a liberty ship that broke in half and rendered another unmanageable. Johnny earned a special commendation from the Commander-in-Chief Home Fleet for taking the helpless *J. H. Latrobe* in tow to safety in Seidisfiord having exhibited superb seamanship against storm force winds and seas.[65] It proved a hazardous business as the broken-down liberty ship had drifted into a minefield after her engines had seized up. Johnny's achievement eventually resulted in the payment of salvage money.[66] *Opportune* caught up with the convoy at Loch Ewe but there was still no rest in sight. She reached Scapa Flow on the 19th and received a four-day boiler clean, but this fell short of the crew's expectation of a 48-hour leave to see families not seen for a long time. The only other small compensation was an opportunity for Johnny's botanists to gather some fauna specimens from the Orkneys, but mostly the ship's company was 'very fed up'.[67]

The 17th flotilla spent the next few months in the Atlantic and Mediterranean, but on 20 August 1943 the destroyers under Johnny's command had the good fortune to escort the carrier *Indomitable* to Norfolk, Virginia, via Bermuda. It was in Bermuda that Johnny discovered one of his relatives was in harbour commanding the yacht *Corsair*, at that time on loan to the Royal Navy. *Corsair*'s role was to patrol Bermudan waters and carry victuals from Trinidad. The victuals included Jamaican rum destined for British ships berthed at Bermuda. Johnny persuaded his relative to fill eleven of *Opportune*'s empty wicker-protected gallon rum jars at the bargain price of 32 shillings and six pence, paid from the wardroom's wine account. Described as 'a special and unexpected asset within a few days in aid of randy full-blooded adventures of three of the 17th DF destroyers' their wardrooms became a focus for much high-spirited partying with members of the opposite sex.

Having delivered the carrier to Norfolk, the crews of *Opportune* and *Obdurate* were disappointed to receive orders to go to Halifax, having hoped for a day to enjoy the recreational facilities of Norfolk's naval base. On 1st September, the two ships left port in stifling heat. Perhaps a sense of disappointment over their forced departure contributed to Johnny's decision to stop the ship just outside the Norfolk Approaches and order the men to bathe. Johnny then led the crew into the water where they spent fifteen minutes splashing around in the cool ocean. This aquatic revelry would undoubtedly have continued but for 'frantic whoops from the destroyer's siren operated by the yeoman drawing the skylarking swimmers' attention to 'shapes emerging from cover of the sea haze'. Bearing down on the stopped and virtually crewless British destroyer was a large US aircraft carrier with her escorts. A mad scramble aboard ensued before a naked and dripping Johnny steered *Opportune* at increasing speed away from the path of the American fleet.[68]

Arriving at Halifax, Johnny received orders to join the escort for the battlecruiser *Renown,* carrying Winston Churchill back to the UK from the Quadrant conference at Quebec. However, for now, the escorts were on standby as the conference overran owing to an extension of the itinerary and the sudden ill health of Dudley Pound, the First Sea Lord. These events allowed *Opportune* and *Obdurate*'s wardroom members to organise ten days of partying that consumed ten of the eleven gallons of *Opportune*'s rum together with a large quantity of other alcohol. The day they sailed, 'many officers and men in the 'O's were feeling worse for wear'.[69] By 17 September, *Opportune* was back with the Home Fleet at Scapa Flow. It was as well that *Opportune* was not in Norfolk that day as a huge explosion from 'ammunition in transit' ripped the naval air base apart, killing at least twenty-four people and injuring a further 250.[70]

Opportune was screening for the American carrier USS *Ranger* when it launched a surprise attack on convoys from the

Norwegian port of Bodø in October1943. Operation Leader did considerable damage to the German war effort by disrupting the transport of iron ore to Germany. At this stage, the Nordland Railway was still under construction and a long way from completion. The precise German losses are hard to ascertain but it seems that three steamers were sunk/destroyed, one troop transport was deemed unrepairable, and six other vessels were beached or otherwise incurred significant damage.[71] The official historian considered the attack an 'outstanding success', noting it was the first combat mission for sixty per cent of the aircrews involved.[72]

Despite the Battle of the Barents Sea mentioned earlier, the continuing presence of *Scharnhorst* and *Tirpitz* in northern waters remained a potent threat to the Arctic convoys. Although eclipsed by her famous sister ship *Bismarck, Tirpitz* probably caused the British more headaches. The role of *Tirpitz* was to act as a 'fleet-in-being' to deter an invasion of Norway. For a variety of reasons she would never make any successful attacks on Allied convoys[73] but the mere possibility of *Tirpitz* intervening against convoy PQ17 had been a major factor in a costly Allied defeat.[74] Despite being immobilised by midget submarines at Altenfjord on 21 September *Tirpitz* was a formidable foe, heavily armoured, carrying a colossal main armament of eight 15-inch guns and capable of turning a decent 29 knots.

Scharnhorst escaped the midget submarines at Altenfjord because she was not in her usual berth. Though less dangerous than *Tirpitz,* she was still a force to be reckoned with carrying nine 11-inch guns directed by radar. *Scharnhorst* already had a bloody reputation, having sunk several merchant ships, and with sister-ship *Gneisenau* shared in the sinking of the armed merchant cruiser *Rawalpindi* and aircraft carrier *Glorious* along with her destroyer escorts during the Norway campaign in 1940. *Scharnhorst* was also a veteran of the celebrated Channel Dash (Operation Cerebus) of February 1942 when German heavy ships from Brest forced their way through the Straits of Dover back to Germany despite several determined air attacks.

In later life, Alec complained that German battleships 'were almost impossible to sink by bombs and gunnery alone. You had to make a big hole under the waterline. Our Torpedo people failed to make this seem important compared with the big gunnery mystique', reflecting a commonly held belief that the 'big gun' lobby and the preponderance of gunnery specialists at the top of the naval hierarchy such as admirals Forbes and his Home Fleet predecessor Roger Backhouse was largely responsible for problems in other branches.[75] Treasury parsimony alongside inter-service rivalry between the Royal Navy and Royal Air Force also played a big part. Indeed, in the 1930s, the Air Ministry decided there was no need to develop bombs larger than 500 lbs and only the experience of war led to the proper development of suitable anti-maritime bombs such as those that finally sank the *Tirpitz* at a very late stage in the conflict.[76]

It would be wrong to think that the Royal Navy was a backward-looking organisation obsessed with the Battle of Jutland in 1916 where the main feature was the big gun duel fought between the opposing fleets. During the inter-war period, the Mediterranean Fleet – the Royal Navy's premier and tactically most influential force – continuously revised and practised their battle tactics. These included the principle of division and sub-division against air and torpedo attack, and critics tend to ignore the difficulties of deciding priorities in an era when guns, torpedoes, bombs, and aircraft were rapidly evolving.[77]

The temporary negation of *Tirpitz* as a potential obstacle was enough to allow the convoys to resume. The Battle of the North Cape on Boxing Day 1943 became the last fight by a British battleship against another battleship and Alec gave a dramatic eyewitness account of the action, firstly on a wartime radio broadcast and later in his memoirs.[78] By now he was first lieutenant of the S-class destroyer *Savage*, under Lt. Commander Michael Meyrick, the son of Alec's former captain at Britannia Royal Naval College.

Alerted by a message from the Operational Intelligence Centre in the early hours of Boxing Day, that *Scharnhorst* was out, *Duke of York*, flagship of the Home Fleet, began stalking the German ship using radar through appalling visibility in the snow and darkness of the Arctic midwinter. The tactics disclosed to Alec, Johnny and their brother officers in the *Duke of York*'s wardroom by Admiral of the Fleet Sir Bruce Fraser were closely adhered too. The plan was to use JW55B as bait to lure *Scharnhorst* towards the British warships, and it was entirely successful. At 16.50, just off Norway's North Cape, *Duke of York* came to within 12,000 yards of the *Scharnhorst* before firing four-star shells that illuminated the target, taking the German completely by surprise. Despite the battleship plunging in waves lashed by gale force winds, *Duke of York* managed to fire a broadside of ten 14-inch guns into the German ship. More salvoes followed, straddling the *Scharnhorst* and forcing her to turn away at high speed, hotly pursued by the British flagship and her accompanying ships. In little more than an hour, *Duke of York* fired 52 broadsides (including 31 straddles) until the *Scharnhorst*'s return fire put the radar out of action. *Scharnhorst* began to pull away and might have escaped altogether but the *Duke of York* repaired her radar and resumed the salvoes.

With the enemy ship now seriously damaged and cut off from her base, Admiral Sir Bruce Fraser signalled for the destroyers to move in. At 18.40 *Savage* and *Saumarez* closed in and scored three torpedo hits on *Scharnhorst*'s port side with *Saumarez* receiving an 11-inch shell hit on her director tower. Several casualties ensued but it did not explode or the consequences would have been far more serious. Both retired under cover of smoke. *Scorpion* and the Norwegian destroyer *Stord* also made a particularly daring attack on the starboard side and scored one torpedo hit. These hits slowed her further and other British ships joined the bombardment. Luckily, for the British, *Scharnhorst*'s radar received damage by a hit from County class cruiser *Norfolk* at an early stage which was unrepairable.

'Much admiration was expressed for the destroyers who pressed home their attack,' recorded the British officers interviewing German survivors, observing how they were 'firing their guns all the time, with great bravery in the face of concentrated fire from *Scharnhorst*'s total armament.'[79] At 19.33 the 71st Sub-Division led by *Musketeer* attacked the German's port side, and at the same time Johnny Lee-Barber in *Opportune* took the 72nd Sub-Division into the attack on her starboard side. They claimed two unobserved torpedo hits and two observed hits. As *Scharnhorst* subsequently 'seems to have taken a list to starboard' the prisoners felt 'that most of the hits were on the starboard side', but the degree of damage inflicted by these sub-divisions is difficult to assess as the cruisers were attacking at the same time and there is no further evidence available.[80] *Scharnhorst* sank around 19.45 with a position recorded as approximately 72°16'N and 28°41'E. The battle proved the value of radar-assisted gunnery as *Scharnhorst* was more than a match for most of her opponents.[81]

Fraser claimed the *Duke of York* was the main factor in the battle, but he also wrote, 'This in no way detracts from the achievements of the "S" class destroyers who with great gallantry and dash pressed in unsupported, to the closest ranges, to deliver their attacks, being subjected the while to the whole fire power of the enemy. Their resolution and skill shortened the battle and ensured the sinking of the ship.'[82] Also singled out was Commander John Lee-Barber, receiving another Mention in Despatches 'For great gallantry, determination and skill while serving in HMS *Opportune*, throughout the action in which the German battleship *Scharnhorst* was sunk.'[83] The wreck found in 2000 turned up in a different location from the reported position above, and investigation revealed that a massive internal explosion blew off her bow, this being why *Scharnhorst* sank so quickly. Only 36 from almost 2,000 crew survived and commander Rear Admiral Erich Bey was not among the survivors. A generally accepted estimate is that 11 out of the 55 torpedoes launched hit their target.[84]

The British made great capital out of the victory. Alec gave a talk for the BBC, and sailors of all ranks and his captain Michael Meyrick gave brief and stilted accounts of the battle for the newsreels.[85] It was a massive psychological blow to the German people as the *Scharnhorst* was a focus of national pride. One downside of the battle for some of the British participants was spending a belated and somewhat restrained post-Christmas celebration at 'miserable Scapa Flow' and there was some envy of the *Musketeer*'s boiler cleans (and leave) at much more amenable Rosyth.[86]

The first months of 1944 meant more Arctic convoying for Johnny's flotilla, and preparations for the planned Operation Overlord, the invasion of France. It was during a boiler-cleaning break in Hull in April 1944 that Johnny lost his beloved Jamie. The death upset Johnny terribly but his friends rallied around and tried to help him by finding a suitable replacement. This proved impossible at short notice but a friend came up with the novel short-term solution of presenting him with two large Aylesbury ducks. This was surprisingly successful and 'Tolley' and 'Cobbold' (named after an East Anglia brewery) found a home on the upper deck. However, the pair was adept at causing confusion among the captains of the other escorts as they tried to comprehend why *Opportune* was not complying with the screen plans. Free to wander the upper and between-decks, the ducks sometimes burned their delicate webbed feet on the hot deck above the engine room. This caused them to hop into the air where crosswinds often blew the pair into the sea. This caused some erratic manoeuvres as Johnny or the officer of the watch turned to place the destroyer up-wind while torpedomen with long poles and large nets prepared to recover Tolley and Cobbold. The ship's company quickly became adept at the recovery drill.[87]

Jamie died shortly before *Opportune* took part in the ill-fated Exercise Tiger, the landing exercise off Slapton Sands in Devon as part of Task Force 27. With the escorts withdrawn in error, German E-boats tore into the landing craft and killed at least 639 sailors and soldiers. *Opportune* engaged the E-boats responsible for the attack but they escaped under cover of smoke. As the exercise was part of a rehearsal for the forthcoming Operation Overlord, the disaster at Slapton was shrouded in secrecy for decades. A few weeks later, Johnny in *Opportune* and Alec in *Savage* were operating on the screen of the invasion fleet off Normandy on D-Day, 6 June 1944, but German naval resistance was slight and, on this occasion, *Opportune* was unable to engage the enemy ships. In the weeks following D-Day there were at least two other occasions in which she engaged E-boats attempting to disrupt the supply lines to Normandy, but they appear to have been inconclusive.[88]

Johnny did not take Tolley and Cobbold with him when Commander R.E.D. Ryder V.C. took over the ship in August 1944. Ryder, a far more conservative and self-contained character than Johnny, must have thought his new subordinates insane. Shortly after taking command, Ryder heard an urgent shout from the bridge. 'I can see it over there, bearing green 60,' yelled the sub-lieutenant. Ryder then heard the first lieutenant ordering an emergency turn for starboard helm and telegraph changes. Rushing to the bridge, in anticipation of imminent combat, the new captain was astonished to see members of his staff 'leaning over steel bridge shields pointing and shouting sighting reports to starboard'. Looking down, he saw his men reaching out with long poles with rings and nets. Gradually, he became aware that all this frantic activity focussed on 'a large white duck valiantly breasting a brisk sea and keeping its head into the wind'. Ryder's reaction is lost to history.[89]

On leaving *Opportune*, his flotilla leader, Captain (Bess) McCoy, described Johnny as a 'V. experienced C.O. of a destroyer who has been a loyal and most successful sub-div. cdr. Has outstanding qualities of leadership. Cool and determined in the face of the enemy.' It seems unlikely that Johnny welcomed it but his countersigning officer suggested that 'A rest ashore after his long and arduous service in destroyers will be beneficial.'[90]

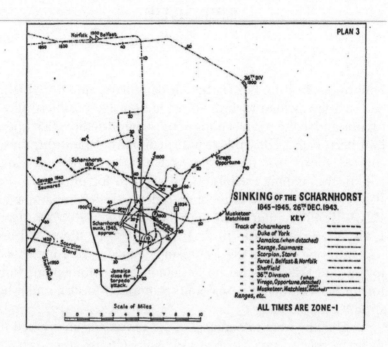

Map

from Despatch on the sinking of the German Battle Cruiser
Scharnhorst 26 December 1943 by Admiral Sir Bruce A.
Fraser, Commander-in-Chief, Home Fleet.

(National Archives, Kew. CAB 106/332).

EPILOGUE

Unfortunately, John Lee Barber, disdainful of paper work to the end, left few written records of his life outside of official files, reports and in the recollections of those naval authors that knew him personally. The limited information available from these sources shows that he served as Executive Officer in King Alfred, the training establishment at Hove for officers of the R.N.V.R., an apt appointment considering his championing of R.N.V.R. officers during his time with *Griffin* and *Opportune*. From 20 October 1948 to 25 January 1950 he impressed his superior officer with his leadership ability, organising skills, loyalty and skills. 'I have no hesitation in recommending him for further command at sea' and 'promotion to Flag rank,' he wrote.[91]

In 1950 he went to Santiago as Naval Attaché and served in the same role at Lima, Bogota, and Quito. Glowing reports from his superiors suggest that his success was in no small measure attributable to Sue's charm and social skills as a hostess alongside his 'excellent work' with the Chilean Navy. So impressed was the government of Chile with 'his untiring work in establishing closer relations between our two Navies' they wished to give him the Military Medal of the Navy, but this was frustrated by Admiralty regulations forbidding the receipt of foreign decorations to Naval Attaches.[92]

He returned to sea commanding the destroyers *St. James* and *Agincourt* and, later, the depot ship *Woolwich*. When Johnny commanded *Agincourt*, Rear Admiral W.G.A. Robson considered him 'unique in the Captains List in his knowledge of the sea and the sailor'. His squadron remained 'the best in the Home Fleet ... He is most strongly recommended for promotion to Flag rank,' Robson wrote.[93] From 1954 to 1957, Johnny was Commodore Harwich, commanding the inshore flotilla; and his final naval appointment, in 1957, was as Admiral Superintendent Malta.

The following year he had the misfortune to have his leg broken during a scuffle with an angry brick-throwing mob from the dockyard. This was ironic considering the Luftwaffe and Kriegsmarine had failed to inflict a single injury upon him in all his years of war service. The riots were over the Admiralty laying off forty Royal Navy Dockyard workers and occurred during Malta's National Day of Protest on 28 April 1958. So serious did they become, the government declared a national emergency and drafted in troops to assist the local police.[94] Given his sincere interest in the Maltese docker's welfare and his robust criticism of the dockyard management regime, Johnny's feelings were deeply hurt over this affair and much sympathy was expressed over his predicament.[95]

It is hard to say to what extent this incident affected his decision to leave the Royal Navy, and a special report of 17 May 1958 on his suitability for retention acknowledged his 'excellent professional knowledge as a practical naval officer'. However, the reporting officer did not think he would 'shine as a staff officer' or in any specialised role such as deciding 'the type of electronic control gear to be fitted in a future guided missile ship.' In fact, Johnny specifically told him 'that he does not particularly want to go on serving after the completion of his present task.'[96] This report anticipated a period of rapid technological change for the Royal Navy and the beginning of the missile age with the first County Class Guided Missile Destroyers already in development. In any case, Johnny was now 64 years of age and too old for the sea-going appointment he would undoubtedly have preferred to have. Rear Admiral John Lee Barber joined the retired list on 29 May 1959 and was appointed Commander of the Bath (C.B.).

After Sue's death from cancer, Johnny retired to Wivenhoe, Essex, to be near his daughters and his sister, Ruth. He was a local celebrity and, in his honour, the town council named a road 'Admiral's Walk' after him in the Wivenhoe Quay development.[97] So popular was the old salt that, to celebrate his 90th birthday, friends honoured him by arranging a special 'fleet review' of local pleasure craft sailing past his house, a kind gesture he much appreciated. Johnny kept in touch with former shipmates, was president of the Russian Convoy Club, and his most prized possession was a pewter tankard presented to him and inscribed with the names of former shipmates. Despite breaking the normally accepted rules of good health regarding smoking and drinking, he lived until the age of 90. It seems doubtful that anyone could have restrained Johnny very much in these matters but his daughter Sarah managed to establish 'a right to veto his interminable fags, at least in the car when I was driving. He could have one half-way to Aunt Ruth's. As we went over the big bridge ... he would always say "Permission to smoke?" and light up.'

Alec's eulogy praised his former captain's thoughtfulness for others, recounting how on a recent visit, and despite ill health, Johnny gave up his bedroom with its magnificent view of the sea simply because he thought Alec would enjoy it. Once he realised Johnny's sacrifice, Alec threatened to stop visiting if he ever tried to do this again.[98]

'In later years, reflecting his more gentle side he acquired whippets. The last was Bockety, a 3 legged whippet from the rescue centre,' wrote Sarah. 'He was the sweetest dog & Pa and I and many in Wivenhoe loved him. Pa was devasted when he died a few years before Pa. He was also devastated when his beloved grand-daughter Clare died in a riding accident aged 21. He never recovered from that and died himself a month later... He loved Victoria and me unconditionally which was a wonderful support.'[99]

Rear Admiral John Lee-Barber had a strong Christian faith that sustained him throughout his life. He is buried with his wife at St. Brelades, Jersey. Walter Stoneman's 1957 photograph of him hangs in the National Portrait Gallery with a copy displayed at the Nottage Maritime Institute on Wivenhoe Quay.

Alec Dennis left *Savage* in late 1944 to take command of the old but modernized V-class destroyer *Valorous* in which he earned another Mention in Despatches for his action in protecting a convoy from a determined E-boat attack in the North Sea, and in May 1945 he was ordered with other ships of the Rosyth Escort Force to help receive the surrender of all German forces at Kristiansand, Norway.

Towards the end of the war, and still an acting half-stripe, he commanded the Hunt-class destroyer *Tetcott* sailing for the Far East where the Japanese seemed intent on fighting to the bitter end. However, the surrender of Japan in August 1945 following the dropping of two atomic bombs meant *Tetcott* got no further than Gibraltar. After the war, Alec served in a number of staff appointments, but as the services gradually returned to peacetime levels, career prospects for younger officers dwindled accordingly. Nevertheless, promoted to Commander in 1953, his professional and personal responsibilities increased. After a few years, and with two young children to consider, he, and his wife started thinking about leaving the Royal Navy and searching for new opportunities abroad. At that time, he was coming to the end of a spell of duty with NATO at its headquarters in Norfolk, Virginia. He explained it thus:

> *On the long car trip back from the west coast, Faith and I had discussed our future. We were not looking forward to returning to our restricted and underpaid life in England. We were still much impressed by the opportunities of life in North America both for ourselves and for our children. I had had my moments of disillusion with the way the Navy, and indeed the country, was going. Chances of distinction were waning and the 'dry list' was really the last straw. So, we thought that I should see what could be done, while on the spot, about finding employment in the U.S.A. or Canada.*[100]

137

Indeed, in the late 1950s, a drastic reorganisation of the U.K.'s defence structure was taking place following Minister of Defence Duncan Sandys' 1957 Defence White Paper placing greater reliance on the hydrogen bomb, missile technology, and making drastic cuts in the navy and air force. This was also the beginning of a process in which the Royal Navy's influence on defence policy diminished by the decision to submerge the role of the Admiralty into a new 'unified' Ministry of Defence in the early 1960s. This gave him the 'final shove', and in 1957, following discussions with friends and relatives, took up the offer of a job in Canada. His final report, covering his time as Head of Drafting Section No. 1, concluded that he had achieved considerable success in difficult circumstances. 'The Royal Navy loses a likeable and efficient officer and I, [Commodore G.B. Rowe] personally lose a most trustworthy supporter.'[101]

After working as a businessman in Montreal, Alec retrained as a teacher and moved to Vancouver where he spent the rest of his life. While there he met and became friends with the former U-boat ace Hans Diedrich von Tiesenhausen, the officer responsible for sinking the battleship *Barham* in November 1941 – an event witnessed by Alec from the deck of his old ship *Griffin*. *Griffin* transferred to the Royal Canadian Navy in 1943 becoming HMCS *Ottawa*. She survived the war but was sold for scrap in August 1946.

On his retirement, Alec's friend, the late Frank Wade, author and veteran of the Royal Canadian Navy, encouraged him to write his wartime memoirs, subsequently lodged in the Imperial War Museum, London, by another friend, the distinguished civil servant John Somerville. Alec was always helpful to historians and kept in touch with former shipmates, making several visits to see Johnny and other friends in the U.K. He outlived his wife and his friend Von Tiesenhausen, dying in 2008 at the age of 90.

APPENDICES

APPENDIX I

STATEMENT BY ALEC DENNIS

POLARES and ENIGMA

It is now 60 years since these events, and more than 30 years since I wrote about them in my memoirs of the war. Recently several things have happened to re-awaken my interest in some aspects of it all.

Firstly, the whole secret business of decyphering the German ENIGMA codes has been made public. At the time of our capture of POLARES we had, of course, no idea of the existence of the ENIGMA machine or of the ULTRA messages which were derived from it.

Secondly, two major books have been published about Bletchley Park, and the captures and decyphering of naval material. The first of these books, by an American, David Kahn, has only the briefest mention of my part in this, but the second, by Hugh Sebag-Montefiore, an Englishman, goes into considerably more detail. Indeed, Hugh S-M 'interviewed' me on the telephone several times after reading my memoir, but I didn't perform very well as I had difficulty hearing him and he had a habit of getting the time difference wrong and I'm not at my best in the small hours. However, he was understanding and did his best to give a fair picture, having also perused the surviving documents in the Public Record Office [The National Archives] at Kew.

Thirdly, the Americans recently produced a wholly fictional and misleading (indeed, dishonest) film [*U-571*, Director J.

Mostow, 2000] portraying the US Navy as the principal captor of the ENIGMA machine, when in fact most of the work had long ago been done by the RN. This film caused something of a furore, and as a result Hugh S-M wrote an article in the London *Times* (1 June 2000) in which for the first time our capture of the POLARES figured prominently.

In his book and article, he did bring out two matters which rather told against me. The first was the fact that I entered Scapa Flow past the assembled fleet flying the White Ensign above the German naval flag[102]. This action was censured by DNI (Director of Naval Intelligence) because, if widely known, it could have given the game away to the Germans that the ship and perhaps the ENIGMA had been captured. The second and rather more serious was that it was reported that POLARES had been 'looted' before the intelligence experts could examine her properly.

As regards the first, at the time it seemed to me to be a time-honoured naval custom from the French, American, and German wars. It never occurred to me that a humble fishing trawler carrying ammunition and stores could be such a valuable intelligence prize. I still think it extraordinary that the Germans should equip such a vulnerable and unimportant unit with a machine whose capture could destroy the secrecy of their entire operations. In any case because the crew were prisoners it would become obvious that the ship had been boarded and not sunk outright like her companion. In spite of all this, it is clear that they never doubted the security of ENIGMA.

The matter of 'looting' is rather more important, and ever since we heard about the accusation, I had felt it to be unfair. However, at the time we were far too busy to give it any thought. But recently, after reading Hugh S-M's book and seeing the references, I sent off to the Public Record Office at Kew for the relevant documents which had remained classified for many years. After a while, a mountain of paper arrived (at considerable cost). I extracted the relevant ones and at last have a good idea of what actually happened. Copies of these are included with this paper.

I have already described the circumstances of the capture in my memoirs, and there is not much that needs altering. I can see that I was under the impression that the trawler carried the original fishing crew. This was not so. I was evidently misled by the fact that many of the naval crew were in civilian fishing gear to keep up their deception. And in the final count of this crew there is no mention of the German army group who were on board. I suppose they were interrogated separately.

As regards the 'looting' accusation, I did indeed allow my small prize crew to take with them some of the abundant eggs and bacon together with some souvenir caps and badges. This did not seem unreasonable. As we lay alongside *Griffin*, Johnny Lee-Barber, rather unwisely as it turned out, allowed many of the ship's company to do likewise. This was supervised by the First Lieutenant, Tony Juniper, and I am quite sure that nothing was broken open at this time and they were limited to the mess deck.

About an hour after we came alongside, a retired Commander appeared and took over from me. Almost his first act was to ask me to find a screwdriver, and proceeded to help himself to a barometer which was fixed to the bulkhead. Thus, his later 'evidence' to the Port Admiral is, to me, highly suspect, although Admiral Binney seems to have trusted him implicitly. He had problems bringing the vessel to an anchor, during which manoeuvre he had some of our men to assist until a scratch crew of minesweeping men took over. It seems likely to me that these people must have done the breaking in which was reported, though the statement of the Sub-Lieutenant (who took over later) denies anything like this. The 'state of chaos' of which much was made was what we found when we captured her. The German crew were surprised and grabbed what they could when we boarded. And the ship had rolled heavily, throwing loose gear all over the place.

It was some weeks later that reports were called for about this state of affairs. Typically, Johnny L-B took all responsibility personally and was kind enough to exonerate me from any blame. He did, however, submit his opinion that POLARES must have been 'considerably rummaged' after leaving *Griffin*. I think he was right. He ended up with 'an expression of Their Lordship's displeasure'. This did not interfere with his successful career in command of destroyers. By this time, we were based at Dover with the German army across the channel so it didn't have much impact, as there was plenty more to think about.

It has taken all these years to identify my villain, a Commander (WSR) F.S. Piper, O.B.E. – a retired Lieutenant (1st April 1913!).

I have included a report of the encounter between HMS *Arrow* and another disguised trawler, *Schiff 37*, which alerted us to the true nature of *Schiff 26* (*POLARES*). In this case the German succeeded in ramming and damaging the destroyer, a courageous act which resulted in the sinking of the trawler by the cruiser *Birmingham* and the loss of all her crew. The poor captain of the *Arrow* also incurred the C in C's displeasure for allowing this to happen; I think I was lucky that Heinz Engelein was not so aggressive as his opposite number.

Well, it's all long ago and history now. But it was adventure at the time.

JAJD, Remembrance Day, 11 November 2001

APPENDIX 11

TNA ADM 199/476

REPORT BY LT. PENNELL RN OF THE N.I.D. 4 MAY 1940.

83

<u>N.I.D. VOL.49. "SECURITY I"</u>

<u>REPORT OF A VISIT TO LYNESS TO INSPECT THE GERMAN PRIZE</u>

<u>TAKEN BY HMS GRIFFIN</u>

I arrived at Kirkwall by air and then proceeded to Lyness where I reported to the Staff Officer, Admiral Commanding Coast of Scotland.

2.   I arrived on board the Prize at about 1700 and after a general inspection, began to make a search for documents, papers etc. This was rendered particularly difficult as the ship appears to have been looted. The following morning, I despatched by air some cypher tables and also sheets of signal pad on which cyphering had been done. These letters were strewn about all over the ship, one sheet being found underneath a mine on the upper deck.

3.   I reported the state of affairs to the Duty Officer N.I.D by telephone and the Admiral Commanding Orkneys and Shetlands and Rear-Admiral Destroyers personally. I requested that every effort should be made to recover all the objects removed from the ship. Among the things stolen were the Captain's private effects, including coats etc., the contents of his

drawers and of his writing case. I was informed by the S.O. (I)'s assistant that in the pocket of one of the coats there was a diary which had been left there to await for my arrival. This coat, however, was missing and I was unable to obtain the diary.

4.   I asked the Admiral Commanding Orkneys and Shetland to have an armed guard placed on board to prevent any further removal of effects etc. A guard of 8 marines from HMS "Iron Duke" was therefore put on board. I was told that a request had already been made to the Rear Admiral, Scapa, to have an armed guard put on board but that it was considered unnecessary.

5.   The Sub-Lieutenant who was in charge of the Prize under the orders of the Port Minesweeping Officer, had done everything that he could do to prevent theft, but locks etc. had been broken during the night. It is probable that his crew, taken from minesweeping drifters did not realise the importance of the papers etc.

6.   Throughout the following day and night, I collected every piece of paper that I could find and separated what might be useful from the remainder and I have brought them back with me. I also arranged, as far as possible, that samples of various pieces of gear should be despatched separately.

7.   The following day a mine was placed on board a trawler, and as the description of it tallied with that of the submarine mine given by prisoners of war, I assisted Lieutenant Glenny, as far as I was able, to render it safe. This delayed my departure until the evening of 2nd May.

8.   No sign was seen of any cyphering machine, but I found the top of the box, which apparently was let into a steel drawer in the wireless cabinet.

9.   The Prize was taken into Kirkwall with the White Ensign over the German flag. I made enquiries to find out how much was known about her, and it is quite certain that practically every rating in the ships at Scapa knows that she has been taken with a great quantity of ammunition, mines, torpedoes etc. on board.

10.   I was also informed that a number of ships had gone alongside for various reasons, and it is probable that they removed small objects as trophies. I was also told that a News Reel photographer from HMS "Repulse" had been on board, but I am not certain whether he actually took any photographs.

(Sgd.) R.G.L. Pennell.

Lieutenant, Royal Navy.

4.5.40.

APPENDIX III

TNA ADM 199/476

REPORT OF COMMANDER PIPER TO REAR ADMIRAL BINNEY 20 MAY 1940

263

SECRET.

To: Admiral Commanding Orkneys and Shetlands, Lyness.

From: Port Minesweeping Officer, Lyness.

Date: May 20th, 1940.

Subject: German Prize taken by HMS Griffin.

      Ref . Admiralty Letter M/N.I.D.001727/40

At 18.30 on Saturday, April 28th, R. A. Scapa gave me short verbal instructions to take a German prize trawler, then alongside HMS Griffin, to a safe anchorage.

2. At 1915 I boarded HMS Griffin, and was informed that an armed boarding crew from the Griffin was in charge, and required to be relieved. I sent away by boat to collect an Officer and crew from M/S trawlers at Long Hope. I then boarded the German trawler Polares, and found R. A. (D). and several senior officers going round the vessel on a tour of inspection.

3. I discussed the vessel and its armaments with Commander Hall Thompson, HMS Rodney, and it was decided, that Vernon, Crombie and the Torpedo Factory at Greenock should be informed immediately of the "find" as I was of the opinion that the mines were magnetic mines laid from tubes, and I did not propose to touch anything till the officials arrived.

4. I then went below, and found the mess-decks littered with gear, lockers smashed open, doors wrenched off, and members of the crew of HMS Griffin taking away every conceivable thing they could carry, and passing them inboard to the Griffin. I instructed a P.O to order the men on deck, and put the hatch doors to, and proceeded down to the engine room, and thence to the Wheel House. From both compartments I ordered men away who were helping themselves to gear etc. I asked the Engineer Officer to make me acquainted with the engines, and I then went on board HMS Griffin and on turning round, found swarms of men from the Griffin still helping themselves to things from the Polares.

5. At about 2000, the C.O. of the Griffin gave me a bunch of keys belonging to the Captain's private apartments in the Polares. I went down below to the apartments and saw they were locked up, and on looking through the grating, the contents looked in order in the sleeping cabin and office. I then also locked the W/T Office and Chart Room, which were in a dreadful mess.

6.   At 2100, signals were passed to me from R.A, (D). To A.C.O.S., and from R.A. Scapa to P.M.S.O., instructing me to take charge, and proceed with the trawler, before dark, to an anchorage. Taking this as a definite order to take over, I asked the First Lieutenant of the Griffin to order all his crew out, and as the relief crew hadn't arrived, I asked them to lend me sufficient hands to steam to an anchorage. I then cast off in the falling darkness and after some difficulties anchored in Myres Bay, clear of all shipping.

7.   At 2130, the Officer and M/S crew arrived alongside, and the Griffin's loaned crew was sent back.

8.   I then took Sub-lieutenant Dutton around the ship, and, gave explicit instructions that nothing had to be touched. They were only required to see she didn't drag or catch fire. No one was to go aft of the bridge, and no fire was to be lit in the galley aft. The Tritonia would lie alongside to assist in case of fire, cook food, etc. These precautionary orders were given because

(i)   abaft the bridge she was a floating arsenal, with mines, depth charges, fused ammunition, etc;

(ii)   the galley was in the compartment leading to the Captain's cabin;

(iii)   by this time the ship was in darkness, as the boilers, etc., had been shut down, and groping about in the dark might cause trouble.

We then locked up every compartment we could find keys for and nailed up others, especially battening doors and nailing up the hatches to the demolition charges – and I took away all the keys.

9.   At 0900, I passed in a written report and copy to R. A. Scapa and A. C. O. S., stating; that "the German trawler had been pillaged by the Griffin before I took over."

10.   At 1100, I visited the trawler again, and in broad daylight, the mess was indescribable. I visited the Captain's quarters, with Sub-Lieutenant Dutton, and we were astounded to see it was broken into and pillaged. I am of the firm opinion that this was done alongside the Griffin as I remember seeing a Sick Berth Attendant with the medical stores just before casting

off and I told him to put them back, and the Medical Officer of the Griffin apologised and had them returned. I found now that the medical stores cupboard was alongside the Captain's cabin door, and the hatchway had to be forced to get down to it, as I had the keys.

11.   I gave definite orders that nothing was to be dumped, just the mess cleared up, as various experts were arriving to examine everything.

12.   I found some papers, which appeared of value, a wallet, an old cap, and a photograph of a destroyer, which I found in the Captain's quarters, and handed them to the D.N.I Representative.

13.   There were some tins of foodstuff and a few bottles of beer found, which I instructed Sub-Lieutenant Dutton to give to the crew.

14.   On arrival of the various experts, every assistance was given them by officers and men of the M/S Flotilla. Lieutenant Commander Cobb, R.N., my Group Officer, volunteered and alone assisted Lieutenant Glenny to render all the mines safe.

15.   At noon on the 2nd of May, by orders of A.C.O.S., an N.C.O. and armed Marine guard was placed on board, with orders that no unauthorised person was permitted to enter the ship.

16.   On the 7th of May, Sub-Lieutenant Dutton and the M/S Flotilla crew and the Marine guard were relieved by Lieutenant Simmonds, R.N. and navigating party, who arrived to take the Polares south.

18.   Attached is report from Sub-Lieutenant W.L.G. Dutton, R.N.R.

J.S. Piper

Commander, R.N.

P.M.S.O

17.   The Polares' defects were made good, she was wiped, and her compasses adjusted, and she sailed 0700 and the 16th of May with the M/S trawler Cape Nyemetzki in company for Liverpool for further refit.

APPENDIX IV

ADM 199/476 75648

REPORT OF SUB-LIEUTENANT DUTTON

266

From: Commanding Officer, German Prize Trawler, and (Sub-Lieutenant W.L.G. Dutton).

To: Port Minesweeping officer, Lyness.

Date: May 2nd, 1940.

I have the honour to submit the following report concerning the above-mentioned vessel: -

2).   During the early evening of Sunday last, April 28th, I received instructions from Lieutenant Commander R. M. Cobb, R.N., Group Commander M/S, to take command of this vessel, and accordingly boarded same in Long hope at 2130 that night, with a scratch, though voluntary crew.

3).   I reported to the P.M.S.O., who was already on board, and later took over from him, he having previously put the ship to single anchor in 8¼ fathoms of water, with four shackles. Upon assuming command, I was instructed to "touch nothing" and was informed that the Chart house, W/T Office and the Commander's Cabin were locked and were not to be interfered with.

4).   Upon making a very preliminary inspection of the vessel generally, I found mess decks and engineer's cabin in a chaotic state. The crew quarters forward was a complete shambles, and the two-berth engineer's cabin abaft but adjoining the messdeck was so ransacked that entry was impossible. The clock on the after bulkhead had been ripped off. The entire living quarters were strewn with beer and spirit bottles, the locker containing same having been broken open and the trap door left lying on deck. Later, 216 bottles were disposed of. This number included 42 lemonade bottles and soda-water bottles.

5).   Small lockers in the mess-deck had been forced open. Both personal gear and clothes were strewn everywhere, large quantities of Danish eggs had been thrown about, and wardrobes, etc., in Officer's cabin were found forced and ullaged (*sic* – pillaged?). Uniform peak caps were found missing and bands and badges of others had been removed. A large quantity of obvious engine room gear (including very necessary spanners, which presumably were at one time on board) could not be found.

6).   At 2205 the same night the second engine room hand reported that no water was shewing in the engine room gauge glass, whereupon I ordered fires to be drawn and electric generator shut down. Watches were set at 2230, and HMS TRITONIA remained alongside throughout the night. One cable was jammed under the gipsy on the windlass and we had no main steam.

7).   Upon P.M.S.O. boarding the following afternoon, entry was made into the Charthouse by means of a key in his possession. Here NO instruments were found except for a local torpedo director. Parallel rules, glasses, telescope, sextant (if any) and even dividers were not to be found. Upon examining the W/T Office a large quantity of paraffin was found on the deck and also some cotton waste was to be seen. A metal box let into the operator's table, probably housing an instrument at some time, was found empty, and no morse key was to be seen, nor was a clock found. Both these compartments were in equally as bad a state as the living spaces the night before:

drawers and lockers were ransacked, and papers later found to be of value to D.N.I. Representative found underfoot.

267

8).   My instructions from **P.M.S.O.** upon his leaving the ship this Monday P.M. were (a) to permit nothing to be touched; and (b) to endeavour to clean up enough of the mess-deck to provide decent living quarters for the crew. Nothing was to be dumped in the way of papers or letters. These instructions I carried out, by locking up papers and books found in the Chart House, and these were handed to the Representative from **D.N.I.**

9).   Tuesday, April 30th, Representatives of A (*sic*) Admiralty departments boarded, and have been given every assistance.[This copy unsigned]Sub-Lieutenant, R.N.R.

APPENDIX V

ADM 199/476

REPORT OF VICE-ADMIRAL BINNEY

262

SECRET

Subject: INSPECTION OF GERMAN PRIZE CAPTURED BY HMS "GRIFFIN"

From: Admiral Commanding, Orkneys and Shetlands, Lyness, Orkney.

Date: 24th May 1940.   No. 510.

To. COMMANDER-IN-CHIEF, HOME FLEET.

The attached reports from the Port Minesweeping Officer who took over the charge of "POLARIS" (*sic*) from the prize crew of HMS "GRIFFIN" and of Sub. Lieutenant Dutton, R.N.R., whom he put in temporary command are forwarded for information with reference to your No. H.F.983/822 of 17th May, 1940.

2.   I wish to state that I have entire confidence in Commander Piper who from the first realised the great importance of this ship and himself personally visited her every day she was at Scapa. I am convinced that no looting was carried out by the officers and men under his command.

3.   On the afternoon of 29th April, I went on board "POLARIS" with Rear Admiral Lyster and walked round the

ship. Our interest was chiefly taken up by examining the various mines, torpedoes, guns and ammunition on board but we did look into the Captain's cabin. I should not describe its state as having been looted. There were a few papers which appeared of no special interest lying about but the cabin appeared to me to have been in the condition it might well have been left in by the original boarding party whom I understand found certain valuable codes and cyphers there. I noticed some of the captain's uniform hanging up and undisturbed. From what I saw I feel convinced that Sub. Lieutenant Dutton and his ship keeping party who were in the drifter alongside had been carrying out their duties properly.

4.   There are certain inaccuracies in Lieutenant Pennell's report.

Paragraph 3. I have been unable to discover to which officer the statement regarding the diary refers. My Staff Officer Intelligence (2) denies all knowledge of it.

Paragraph 4. I have been unable to check the statement that the Rear Admiral, Scapa did not consider an armed guard was necessary as the then Rear Admiral is now in the Narvik area. He did however give directions that no one was to be allowed on board without written authority from himself (message 1858 of 30th April, 1940). A Royal Marine guard was placed on board by my orders on 1st May, 1940.

Paragraph 9. The prize was not taken to Kirkwall but to Scapa and the correct procedure was adopted as regards flags and ensigns. Whilst it is impossible to keep secret in the base itself knowledge of the ship and what she carried on board; I think that any real knowledge was confined to very few personnel.

Paragraph 10. No ships other than "TRITONIA" went alongside and only such boats as were essential.

5.   Lieutenant Pennell came to see me in the morning of 1st May. He was very tired after his all-night search of the "POLARIS" and rather over-wrought. I think this condition coloured his report. He informed me that the "GRIFFIN" had done a lot of looting and I sent him off to Rear Admiral (D) to report.

6.   In fairness to all concerned I think it should be pointed out that the original Boarding Party had taken from the ship certain codes and cyphers and that it was generally assumed that all documents which might be of value to Director of Naval Intelligence had already been dealt with.

T H Binney,

VICE-ADMIRAL

APPENDIX VI

ADM 199/476

LT. COMMANDER LEE-BARBER'S REPORT TO ADMIRAL FORBES

FROM.... THE COMMANDING OFFICER, HMS "GRIFFIN".

DATE.... 25th JUNE 1940.
        No.001/PO/30.

TO.... THE COMMANDER-IN-CHIEF, HOME FLEET.

_____

Submitted,

With reference to your memorandum No. H.F.983/949 dated 30th May 1940, I have held an investigation into this matter and the following report is forwarded.

2.   When the prize came alongside "GRIFFIN" the messdeck and enclosed compartments generally were in an untidy state, this was partly due to the fact that during the passage to Scapa the ship was rolling heavily, and partly that the 12 prisoners who were transferred at sea on the evening of the 26th April were permitted a very short time to collect their gear from the messdeck before being transferred. The seven prisoners who came in with the ship were allowed below to pack their gear before coming alongside "GRIFFIN" and were put onboard "GRIFFIN" immediately the prize was secured. Lieutenant Dennis reports that numerous empty bottles were on the mess deck when the ship was captured.

3.   Lieutenant Dennis further reports that he could not find any navigational instruments when he took over the prize and

that he had to use a set square as parallel ruler. Lieutenant Engelion (*sic*), the Commanding Officer of "POLARES" came aboard "GRIFFIN" wearing a pair of binoculars, these he gave to Surgeon Lieutenant J.G. Walley, R.N.V.R. One other member of the crew of "POLARES" also had a pair of binoculars when he came aboard and these were taken from him and have been added to the stock of instruments onboard "GRIFFIN" which is considerably below establishment.

4.   I do not consider that any blame can be attached to the prize crew who brought "POLARES" in.

5.   From my investigation and from my own personal observation when I went onto the messdeck of "POLARES" whilst she was alongside, I am convinced that no cases of breaking open lockers or removing gear other than that mentioned in my previous report in paragraphs 4 and 5 took place. The removal of the stores mentioned in paragraph 5 was done under the direct supervision of my Executive Officer, Lieutenant W.A. Juniper, and the storeroom was then locked up.

6.   I respectfully submit that there can be no grounds for a charge of gross indiscipline against the ship's company of HMS "GRIFFIN" and that the full responsibility for the removal of such things as were taken must rest ... [text illegible].

270

I realize that in allowing my ship's company to board and take away souvenirs from the prize I committed an error of judgement and contravened the Naval Discipline Act.

7.   I further submit that I am convinced that "POLARES" must have been considerably rummaged after leaving HMS "GRIFFIN" for the state she was reported to have been in the next day to have been possible.

J. Lee-Barber.

LIEUTENANT COMMANDER

 IN COMMAND.

APPENDIX VII

TNA ADM 199/476

SIGNAL FROM FORBES TO ADMIRALTY, 30 JUNE 1940 <u>SECRET</u>

C. in C. Home Fleet to Secretary of the Admiralty, 30 June 1940.

SUBJECT: INSPECTION OF PRIZE "POLARES"
Forwarded for information with reference to Admiralty letter M/M.I.D.00172740 of 14th May, 1940.

2. It is difficult to reach a just conclusion on this matter, the evidence of the two sides being so divergent. It seems that some part of the disorder found by Commander Piper on taking over the prize may have been due to the actions of the German crew before they left the ship. Nevertheless, I do not consider that the Commanding Officer and ship's company of HMS Griffin can be freed from all blame.

3. I have ordered the Commanding Officer of HMS Griffin to return both pairs of binoculars to the Superintending Naval Store Officer of the nearest dockyard and to report when he has done so.

4. As the Commanding Officer, HMS Griffin absolves from blame the members of the Prize Crew who brought the ship in, I am forwarding separately the recommendations for awards to these officers and men, on which I had suspended judgement.

C. M. Forbes, Admiral of the Fleet

BIBLIOGRAPHY

Books

Bacon R.H.S., *The Dover Patrol, 1915-1917*. New York, George H. Doran Company, 1919.

Bacon R.H.S., *Britain's Glorious Navy*. Odhams, 1942.

Bennett R., *Behind the Battle: Intelligence in the War with Germany, 1939-45*. Pimlico, 1999.

Cato, *Guilty Men*. Gollancz, 1940.

Churchill W.S., *The Gathering Storm Vol.1 of the Second World War*. Penguin Classics, 1983.

Connell G.G., *Arctic Destroyers: The 17th Flotilla*. Wm. Kimber & Co, 1982.

Cook C. & Stevenson M., *The Longman Handbook of Modern European History 1763-1991*. Longman, 1992.

Cumming A. J. (ed), *In Action with Destroyers: The Wartime Memoirs of Commander J.A.J. Dennis D.S.C., R.N.,* Barnsley: Pen & Sword Maritime, 2017.

Divine D., *The Broken Wing: A Study in the British Exercise of Air Power*. Hutchinson, 1966.

English J., Amazon *to Ivanhoe: British Standard Destroyers of the 1930s*. World Ship Society, 1993.

Fiennes J., *Britannia's Voices: Sixty Years of Training at Dartmouth*. Gomer Press, 2017.

Greene J. & Massignani A., *The Naval War in the Mediterranean, 1940-1943*. Annapolis, MD: Naval Institute Press, 2011.

Griehl M., *Junkers JU.87 Stuka*. Shrewsbury: Airlife Publishing, 2001.

Herman A., *To Rule the Waves: How the British Navy Shaped the Modern World*. Hodder & Stoughton, 2005.

Hinsley F.H., Thomas, E.E, Ransom C.F.G. and Knight R.C., *British Intelligence in the Second World War. Vol.1. Its Influence on Strategy and Operations*. HMSO, 1979.

Ireland B., *History of Ships*, Hamlyn, 1999

Ranson E., British *Defence Policy and Appeasement between the Wars, 1919-1939*. The Historical Association, 1993.

Jianguo Z. & Junyong Z., *Weihaiwei Under British Rule: Weihai (Weihaiwei) Twinned with the British Town of Cheltenham*. Reardon Publishing, 2007.

Kemp P., *Convoy: Drama in Arctic Waters*. Minneapolis: Book Sales Inc., 2004.

Lavery B., *Churchill's Navy: The Ships Men and Organisation 1939-1945*, Conway 2006.

Miller D., *Warships from 1860 to the Present Day*. Greenwich Editions, 2004

Morris T.A., *European History, 1848-1945*, Harper Collins, 1996.

Roskill S., *The Navy at War 1939-1945*, Wordsworth Military Library, 1998

Roskill S., *The War at Sea, 1939-45*, HMSO, 1954

Sebag-Montefiore H., *Enigma: The Battle for the Code,* Weidenfeld & Nicolson, 2000 & 2018 edns.

St. Hill Bourne D., *They Also Serve.* Winchester Publications, 1947.

Wardle H., *Forecastle to Quarterdeck: Memoirs 1939-1945*, CPW Books, Hayling Island, 1994.
Williamson G., *German E-boats 1939-45* Bloomsbury, 2012.

Archives

Churchill Archives, Cambridge.
CA ROSK Papers of Captain S.W. Roskill.

Ministry of Defence, London
Service records of Rear Admiral John Lee-Barber C.B., D.S.O., R.N., and Commander J.A. Dennis D.S.C., R.N.

The National Archives, Kew
TNA ADM 1. Admiralty and Ministry of Defence, Navy Department.
TNA ADM 199. Admiralty: War History Cases and Papers Second World War, 1922-1968.
ADM 223. Admiralty: Naval Intelligence Reports and Papers , 1914-1978
CAB 120. Ministry of Defence Secretariat.

Naval History Websites

Arnold Hague Convoy Database: convoyweb.org.uk
Naval History.Net: naval-history.net
U-boat.Net: uboat.net V&W Destroyer Association:
vandwdestroyerassociation.org.uk/HMS
Woolston/Bergen.html
Wrecksite: wrecksite.eu

Other Websites

The Comprehensive Guide to the Victoria and George Cross:
vconline.org.uk
BBC History: bbc.co.uk/history
The Guardian: theguardian.com
HyperWar Foundation: ibiblio.org
The Independent: independent.co.uk
The London Gazette: thegazette.co.uk
The Times of Malta: timesofmalta.com
NavWeaps: navweaps.com
NavyLive:navylive.dodlive.mil/2013/01/25/mast-stepping-a-
mariners-tradition
New York Times: nytimes.com
University of Wisconsin-Madison Libraries:
digital.library.wisc.edu
Revolvy: revolvy.com
War History Online: warhistoryonline.com
World War II Unit Histories &Officers: unithistories.com
Wayback Machine: web.archive.org
Rear-Admiral John Lee-Barber, Wivenhoe Encyclopedia:
wivencyclopedia.org/History/Lee-Barber.htm
(accessed 30 October 2018)

Periodicals

Bennett G.H., 'The Arctic Convoys: The Worst Journey in the World', *BBC History Magazine*, pp.50-56.

Hore P., 'Guns who Played Key Part in Royal Navy's last Battleship Fight', *Warships International Fleet Review,* June 2016, p.45.

Rear Admiral John Lee-Barber, Obituaries, *Daily Telegraph*, 22 November 1995, p.15.

Lashmar P., 'The true story of the ENIGMA capture', *Independent*, 16 March 2000, p.10-11.

Levy J., 'Lost Leader: Admiral of the Fleet, Sir Charles Forbes'. The Mariner's Mirror 88. No.2 (2002): 190.

Naval Station Norfolk Explosion, *New York Times*, 18 September 1943. p.19.

Sumida J.T., 'The Best Laid Plans: The Development of British Battle Fleet Tactics, 1919-1942', International History Review 14, no. 4, (1992): 681-700.

Sebag-Montefiore H., 'The Crucial Capture', *Times*, 1 June 2000, pp.3-4.

NOTES

[1] The life and training of Dartmouth's officer cadets from the 1930s onwards is covered in Fiennes J, *Britannia's Voices: Sixty Years of Training at Dartmouth* (Gomer Press Ltd., 2017).

[2] ETHIOPIAN COURT HEARS HOW EMPEROR WAS KILLED, *The Washington Post*, washingtonpost.com/archive/politics/1994/12/15/ethiopian-court-hears-how-emperor-was-killed/af51020c-547c-4b9c-92df-52be6e2a2241/?noredirect=on&utm_term=.877e7e11617b (accessed 14 March 2019).

[3] Malta and the Spanish Civil War, Times of Malta, timesofmalta.com/articles/view/20161106/life-features/Malta-and-the-Spanish-Civil-War.630207 6 Nov.2016. (accessed 17 Janary 2018).

[4] His great-grandfather was one of the sailors escorting Napoleon into exile to Elba.

[5] When stopping or going very slow the prop acts like a paddle and pushes the stern to one side. Hence you try and get the boat or ship's stern to swing the opposite way when going alongside.

[6] and a controversial director of the National Trust.

[7] Zhang Jianguo & Zhang Junyong, *Weihaiwei Under British Rule: Weihai (Weihaiwei) Twinned with the British Town of Cheltenham* (Reardon Publishing, 2007).

[8] Nanjing massacre: China's Xi Jinping leads first state commemoration, BBC, bbc.co.uk/news/world-asia-30460818 (viewed 30 May 2019).

[9] Foreign Relations of the United States, University of Wisconsin-Madison Libraries, http://digital.library.wisc.edu/1711.dl/FRUS (accessed 31 May 2019).

[10] An address by Captain Michael Hennessy at the Service of Thanksgiving for the Life of John Lee-Barber.

[11] Yangtze Patrol, Revolvy, revolvy.com/page/Yangtze-Patrol (accessed 21 August 2018).

[12] Letter from J Lee Barber to his family, from *Falcon* at Chungking, 12 July 1932.

[13] Wardle H, *Forecastle to Quarterdeck: Memoirs 1939-1945* (CPW Books, Hayling Island 1994), pp.28-31. Corticene was a type of linoleum fastened to the deck by brass strips.

[14] Jamie died in 1941. St. Hill Bourne D, *They Also Serve* (Winchester Publications, 1947), p.96.

[15] Letter from Sarah Lee-Barber and telephone conversation with author on 8th August 2019.

[16] English J, *Amazon to Ivanhoe: British Standard Destroyers of the 1930s* (World Ship Society, 1993). p.89 &141.

[17] Confidential report on Lt. John Lee-Barber by Lt. Cmdr R Swinley, 26 April 1927-19 April 1929, dated 20 April 1929.

The countersigning officer was Captain (later Admiral) Tom Phillips who went down with the *Prince of Wales* in late 1941.

[18] Confidential reports by Capt (D) G Creasey, 31 March 1940 & 16 May 1940, Capt. De Winton, 8 November 1940, J A Mack, 14 March 1941 & 27 December 1941, J.A. McCoy, 24 August 1944

[19] Connell G G., *Arctic Destroyers: The 17th Flotilla*, (Wm. Kimber & Co Ltd, 1982), pp.91-2.

[20] Alec Dennis's address at the Service of Thanksgiving for the life of Rear Admiral John Lee-Barber CB, DSO, held at St Mary the Virgin, Wivenhoe on 15 January 1996.

[21] Holland J, *Fortress Malta: An Island under Siege, 1940-1943*, (Orion, 2003), p.20.

[22] Cumming A (ed.) *In Action with Destroyers 1939-1945, The Wartime Memoirs of Commander J. A. J. Dennis* (Pen & Sword Maritime 2017)

 p.7. Mess undress in 1939 was one of three forms of formal eveningwear worn by RN officers. It consisted of plain trousers, mess jacket, blue waistcoat, black bow tie, and formal white shirt.

[23] Richmond H., in Bacon R, *Britain's Glorious Navy*, (Odhams, 1942), p.17.

[24] Ireland B, *History of Ships*, (Hamlyn, 1999), p.69.

[25] Lashmar P, 'The true story of the ENIGMA capture', *Independent,* 16 March 2000, pp.1-5.

[26] Mason G B, Entry for HMS *Arrow*, H42 A-Class Destroyer, "Service Histories of Royal Navy Warships in World War 2", naval-history.net/xGM-Chrono-10DD-13A-Arrow.htm (accessed 19 February 2018).

[27] Lee-Barber to Rear Admiral (D) HMS Woolwich. Capture of German Trawler – Enclosure No.1, Commanding Officer, HMS Griffin's report at Scapa Flow, 5 May 1940. Ibid, 256

[29] Lee-Barber to Rear Admiral (D) HMS Woolwich. Commanding Officer, HMS Griffin's report at Scapa Flow, 5 May 1940.

[30] Interview with J.A.J Dennis by H Sebag-Montefiore in 1998 in Sebag-Montefiore H, *Enigma: The Battle for the Code,* Weidenfeld & Nicolson, 2000, p.74, & endnote 9, p.366.

[31] Note made by Dennis on Heinz Engelein's notepaper, undated but apparently April 1940.

[32] The National Archives (TNA) ADM 199/476 75648 Lee-Barber to C.in.C. Home Fleet, 'Inspection of Prize "Polares", 25 June 1940.

[33]. Sebag-Montefiore H, 'The Crucial Capture', *Times,* 1 June 2000, pp.3-4

[34] Dennis J A J, Note on Polares and Enigma, Remembrance Day, 11 November 2001, pp.1-3.

[35]TNA ADM 199/476 From Admiral J Godfrey, Capture of Prize "Polares". D.N.I., N.I.D., Vol.49. "SECURITY I" N.I.D. 001727/40 of 4.5.40.

[36] Sebag-Montefiore, *Times,* pp.3-4.

[37] Dennis, Polares and Enigma, 11 Nov.2000, p.2.

[38] TNA ADM 199/476 Report of Commander Piper to Rear Admiral Binney, 20 May 1940.

[39] TNA ADM 199/476 Report by Vice Admiral T. H. Binney to Admiral of the Fleet, Sir Charles Forbes, 24 May 1940.

'Inspection of German Prize Captured by HMS "Griffin".

[40] TNA ADM 199/476 Report by Lt. Pennell of the N.I.D., 4 May 1940.

[41] Report by Vice Admiral T.H. Binney to Admiral of the Fleet, Sir Charles Forbes, 24 May 1940. 'Inspection of German Prize Captured by HMS "Griffin".'

[42] TNA ADM 199/476 75648 Lee Barber to Admiral Forbes, 25 June 1940.

[43] Sebag-Montefiore H, *Enigma: The Battle for the Code*, (Weidenfeld & Nicolson, 2018), pp. 490-1. Readers who wish to delve into this in greater detail should read the personal accounts including reports by Admirals Binney and Forbes.

[44] Alec's memoirs singled out Hinsley F.L. *et al.*, *British Intelligence in the Second World War*. Vol 1. (HSMO, 1979).
[45] Sebag-Montefiore, *Times*, p.3.

[46] Mahon A P., The History of Hut Eight, Graham Ellsbery.com p.22 ellsbury.com/hut8/hut8-000.htm (accessed 23 February 2018).

[47] Sebag-Montefiore, *Enigma*, p.3.

[48] Lieutenant Commander David Balme – Obituary, *Daily Telegraph* telegraph.co.uk/obituaries/2016/03/18/lieutenant-commander-david-balme---obituary/ (accessed 29 April 2019).

[49] Entry for John Lee-Barber, Traces of War, tracesofwar.com/persons/74874/Lee-Barber-John.htm (accessed 29 April 2019).

[50] To be Companions of the Distinguished Service Order for 11 July 1940 : Lieutenant Commander John Lee Barber, *London Gazette,* 9 July 1940, p.4257. thegazette.co.uk/London/issue/34893/supplement/4257

Mention in Despatches, 19 July 1940, 4492
thegazette.co.uk/London/issue/34901/supplement/4492

[51] Letter from Sarah Lee-Barber.

[52] MOD, Southern Cmd, Army HQ (NLO) Service record
entry for 13th August 1942, Capt. Norris. .

[53] Connell G G, *Arctic Destroyers: The 17[h] Flotilla* (Wm.
Kimber & Co Ltd., 1982) p..92.

[54] Miller D, *Warships from 1860 to the Present Day*
(Greenwich Editions, 2004) p.376.

[55] Churchill probably borrowed the phrase from the title of
Apsley Cherry-Garrard, *The Worst Journey in the World:
Antarctica 1910-1913* (first published in 1922. Books on
Demand, 2010).

[56] Bennett G H, 'The Arctic Convoys: The Worst Journey in
the World', *BBC History Magazine*, pp.50-56.

[57] Roskill S, *The Navy at War 1939-1945*, (Wordsworth
Military Library, 1998) pp.207-8

[58] Entry for Commander Manley Power,
uboat.net/allies/commanders/2037.html (accessed 3
September 2018).

[59] BR 1736 (53) 2 *Naval Staff History: The Development of
British Naval Aviation 1919-1945* Vol.2. (Admiralty, London,
1956), p.299.

[60] Connell, *Arctic Destroyers*, p. 104.

[61] Connell, *Ibid*, p. 110.

[62] From Paul Hartwig to Lee-Barber, 14 Dec. 1995.

[63] Connell, Arctic Destroyers, pp.116-17.

[64] Roskill, *The Navy*, 271-2.

[65] Connell *Arctic Destroyers*, p.139.

[66] Entry for HMS *Opportune*, 10 March 1943 naval-history.net/xGM-Chrono-10DD-47O-HMS_Opportune.htm (accessed 16 May 2019)

[67] Connell, *Arctic Destroyers*, pp. 138-9.

[68] Connell, *Ibid*, 153-5

[69] Connell, *Ibid*, 154-5

[70] Naval Station Norfolk explosion, *New York Times*, 18 September 1943. p.19.

[71] A Glimmer of Hope: Remembering Operation Leader

4 October 1943, Naval History and Heritage Command, history.navy.mil/browse-by-topic/wars-conflicts-and-operations/world-war-ii/1943/operation-leader.html (accessed 17 May 2019)

[72] Roskill S, *The War at Sea*, III (HMSO, 1954) p.102.

[73] Roskill, *The Navy*, 318-24.

[74] Roskill, *Ibid*, 207-9.

[75] E-mail from Alec Dennis to author, 1 February 2007.

[76] Divine D, *The Broken Wing: A Study in the British Exercise of Air Power* (Hutchinson, 1966) 190-1.

[77] Sumida,"The Best Laid Plans", *International History Review*.14. No.4 (1992) 681-700.

[78] There is a radio broadcast on YouTube that may possibly represent the text of Alec's broadcast but his children do not recognise the narrator's voice. Scharnhorst - HMS Savage (5 January 1944)

youtube.com/watch?v=jNG5AiM7lWk (accessed 15 May 2019)

[79] TNA ADM 1, 6833 Sinking of Scharnhorst, Report of Director of Naval Intelligence, 16 Jan. 1944, Enclosing Information Obtained from Prisoners of War, ex Scharnhorst, 1st January 1944.

[80] *Ibid*, para 75, p.3709

[81] Hore P, 'Guns Who Played Key Part in Royal Navy's last Battleship Fight', *Warships International Fleet Review*, June 2016, p.45.

[82] TNA ADM1 Sinking of Scharnhorst, para 81-3, p.3710. Also see Admiral Bruce Fraser's Despatch, Sinking of the German Battlecruiser *Scharnhorst* on the 26th December 1943. Supplement to the *London Gazette* of 5 August 1947, pp. 3703-10.
ibiblio.org/hyperwar/UN/UK/LondonGazette/38038.pdf (accessed 17 May 2019)

[83] Statement of Service of Rear Admiral John Lee-Barber CB DSO. 1942-44. Ministry of Defence.

[84] The Sinking of the Scharnhorst, bbc.co.uk/history/worldwars/wwtwo/scharnhorst_01.shtml#four (accessed 25 July 2018)

[85] Commander of HMS Savage, British Pathé, youtube.com/watch?v=W4Rmh0WzCNs (accessed 25 July 2018)

[86] Cumming, IAWD, p.143.

[87] Connell, *Arctic Destroyers*, p.179.

[88] Entries for *Opportune*, 28 April, 27 July and 17 August 1944, naval-history.net/xGM-Chrono-10DD-47O-HMS_Opportune.htm (accessed 17 May 2019)

[89] Connell, *Arctic Destroyers*, 184.

[90] MOD Service Record Opportune C.O. Entry for 14 August 1944, Capt. McCoy and Cdre. Hutton.

[91] MOD Report by Vice-Admiral A.R.M. Bridge, Flag Officer Commanding Reserve Fleet, 3 Feb. 1950.

[92] MOD From C.N. Stirling, British Embassy, Santiago to Rt. Hon Anthony Eden, M.P., 18 May, 1952, enclosing letter from Chilean Ministry of Defence, 2 May 1952.

[93] MOD Supersession of Flag Officer 11 August 1952 - 30 July 1953 by Rear-Admiral W.G.A. Robson.

[94] Medical Officer of the Malta Garrison – 1958 maltaamc.com/regsurg/re1950/rmo1958.html (accessed 10 September 2018)

[95] From the Office of the First Sea Lord to Lee-Barber, 10 April 1959. However, a telephone conversation with Johnny's

daughter Sarah suggests he may have had a knee injury rather than a broken leg.

[96] MOD Report by Admiral C E Lambe, C.in.C. Mediterranean, 17 May 1958.

[97] Rear-Admiral John Lee-Barber, *Wivenhoe Encyclopedia,* wivencyclopedia.org/History/Lee-Barber.htm (accessed 30 October 2018)

[98] Eulogy by Alec Dennis at Service of Thanksgiving for the Life of John Lee-Barber

[99] Letter from Sarah Lee-Barber.

[100] E-mail from Alec Dennis to author, 1 February 2007.

[101] MOD Termination of Appointment Report for J A J Dennis by Commander W E Messenger and Commodore G B Rowe, 1 Dec. 1957.

[102] signifying this was a captured ship.

Erratum

Pages 103, 167, 177
Hennessy, should be Hennell.

Index

Ships & Boats

American

British

180